Teaching Assistants' Box of Tricks

Successful and engaging strategies for science teaching assistants

Jo Foster

with Sarah Van Baalen

The **Association**
for **Science Education**
Promoting Excellence in Science Teaching and Learning

The author and publisher would like to acknowledge the following for material reproduced in the book.

Extracts adapted from National Strategies: Framework for teaching Secondary Science – Overview and learning objectives
© Crown copyright

Extracts adapted from National Strategies: materials developed from an original idea from Progressing to Level 6 and Beyond
© Crown copyright

QCA
Programme of Study for Science KS2
Programme of Study for Science KS3
Programme of Study for Science KS4

Graduate into Employment Unit: *The art of building windmills – Career tactics for the 21st Century*

The author and publishers would like to thank the staff and pupils at Camborne Science and Community College, Camborne for permission to reproduce the photographs that appear in the book.

First published 2009
Reprinted 2009

Published by The Association for Science Education
College Lane, Hatfield, Herts AL10 9AA
Telephone: 01707 283000
Email: info@ase.org.uk
Website: www.ase.org.uk

ISBN 978 0 86357 421 4

Designed by Colin Barker
Printed by A C Print Solutions Hunsdon, Herts

Association for Science Education

The Association for Science Education is the professional body for science teachers and others contributing to science education at all levels in the United Kingdom. ASE is committed to the advancement of science education and provides specialist journals, publications, meetings, advice and support for all those involved in teaching science. ASE publications are written by ASE members to provide advice, support and relevant information on key science education issues to ASE members and others involved in science education. ASE members enjoy significantly lower prices on all ASE publications. To find out more visit **www.ase.org.uk**

Contents

'I not only use all the brains that I have, but all that I can borrow.'

Woodrow Wilson

Acknowledgments

I am indebted to the many teachers, teaching assistants and students who have shared their ideas, experiences and views with me during the writing of this book. I have been privileged to have spent much of the past two years in other people's classrooms, watching and learning from the interactions between staff, pupils and teaching assistants. I hope that I have managed to capture some of that best practice in this publication, and I also hope that I have provided some solutions for those teachers and teaching assistants who are struggling to work together in the most effective way to support student learning.

Special thanks to Sarah Van Baalen, an inspirational Higher Level Teaching Assistant from Camborne Science and Community College, who has been a great source of insight, enthusiasm and ideas while I've been writing this book.

Huge appreciation and thanks to Ed Walsh, Cornwall Science Advisor, who has, as ever, been a brilliant sounding board for my ideas, and has been an amazing mentor to me since he first came into my classroom to watch me teach four years ago. He also carried out superhuman editorial duties during pretty much the only week he'd had off in six months.

I am also extremely grateful to my marvellous husband, John for putting up with my hours in front of the computer writing while he made sure that life in general continued to run smoothly around me. John, you're my hero.

Jo Foster

'Act as if what you do makes a difference. It does.'

William James

Preface

This is a book for teachers and for teaching assistants. It is designed to give teaching assistants engaging activities that help them to support the students whether or not, initially, there is guidance from the teacher. The ideas and strategies can be freely shared between teachers and teaching assistants – they will be most effective if they become part of the everyday support available to learners in your classrooms.

You may already be working extremely effectively in partnership with a very supportive teacher or science department. That's great, and the strategies in the book will be helpful in moving your support up a gear.

Conversely, as a teaching assistant reading this, you may be thinking, 'How can I be effective if the teacher doesn't tell me what he wants me to do?' The only place to start is where you are. As a teaching assistant, you might like clear direction given each lesson about the sort of support to provide, but if this is not forthcoming, there is still plenty that you can do to support students in their learning.

As a teacher reading this, you may be thinking, 'I have so much to do already – I don't have time to tell someone else how to do the job!' Once you start to work more effectively with your teaching assistant, you will be amazed how the learning moves on in your classroom. Part of this is about giving the teaching assistant the opportunity to shine, and showing that you are confident that you can improve learning in your classroom together.

Or, as a teacher, you may be looking at this book wondering whether to buy it as a gift for the fabulous teaching assistant you are working with in your classroom or department. Please do so; the strategies and ideas in this book will help you both.

Jo Foster
2009

'Restlessness and discontent are the first necessities of progress.'

Thomas Edison

Chapter 1
Where are we now?

Objectives

■ To explore some of the reasons why teaching assistants are not used as effectively as they might be.

I would hazard a guess that almost all science labs have unused resources in them. In most labs there is at least one 'no go' area, where dusty, rusty, old, once indispensable artefacts gently turn to dust. But what if those artefacts at the back of the cupboard could be dusted off and used to enrich and enhance your teaching? What if the rusting, forgotten, ignored equipment was the very thing that could enormously enhance the progress of your pupils, provide information and ideas on how to move on some of your most difficult pupils, and make your job easier and more satisfying? Would you use it? Of course you would!

I am not for one moment suggesting that teaching assistants are either dusty or rusty – but I am suggesting, based on many conversations with teaching assistants, pupils and teachers, that they are a profoundly under used resource.

Why is there a need for this publication?

During my classroom practice as a science teacher and subsequently as a science Advanced Skills Teacher, I was sorely aware that, though I tried hard to work with my teaching assistant as much and as effectively as possible, there were times when I failed, and failed miserably. There were many reasons for this, but not many excuses. As a fellow professional, in the classroom to help the learners move forward, it is part of a teacher's professional role to work with the teaching assistant appropriately. The induction standards require that the newly qualified teacher can *'work effectively as part of a team and as appropriate to the post in which they are completing induction, liaise with, deploy, and guide the work of other adults who support pupil's learning'*.

The way this book is written

I have drawn on current practice in schools; from both my own classroom and those of others, for much of this book. I have also had extensive conversations with teaching assistants, higher level teaching assistants, school leaders, consultants and advisors about the issues that surround teaching assistants and their effective use. I have drawn on the experiences of many teachers and teaching assistants who have participated in workshops and courses that I have run both in Cornwall and nationally on the effective use of teaching assistants.

For the writing of this chapter in particular, I have compared my own experiences and supported my own suggestions of good practice with ideas put forward through research that has been published in this area. Where a statement has been backed up by a research project or other published work, the authors of the work are mentioned in the text and the date of the publication given after the author names. If you wish to find out more or to read the studies in more detail, the references can be found in the Bibliography, see page 118.

What experience and research tells us

The expectation is that teaching staff will guide and support the teaching assistants they work with. In my experience this is not always the case, and even when some guidance is given, it may not be entirely helpful. Teaching assistants sometimes express frustration at feeling underused and unappreciated by the teaching staff they work with. Many teaching assistants identify a lack of time to plan or work with teachers as a problem; 44% of the 1560 higher level teaching assistants (HLTAs) surveyed by Wilson *et al.* (2007) said that this lack of time was a block to effective working. A lack of planning time may be a reason for the limited impact of teaching assistants on pupil learning in primary classrooms (Blatchford *et al.*, 2002; Blatchford *et al.*, 2004; Gerber *et al.*, 2001). However, there is some good news; a literature review by Howes *et al.*, (2003) confirmed that teaching assistants did have an impact on the test scores of individual pupils, though not on the whole-class outcomes. The same review also highlighted that teaching assistants can prevent the pupils they are supporting from engaging with other pupils and the classroom teacher – clearly not a helpful outcome. One way to ameliorate this is, and to spread the benefits of teaching assistant support more widely than just an individual pupil, might be to support pupils in small groups. This book explores a number of ways that the teaching assistant can support small groups.

Often, teaching assistants receive little training in how to effectively support learning, and teachers receive little training in how to support teaching assistants (Cajkler *et al.*, 2007).

My aim is to help teachers and teaching assistants work more effectively together to move learning on for everyone in the class. I think this needs a new approach – an acceptance that, though teachers and teaching assistants do need time to work together on planning and evaluation, they often do not get it. Though it would be great if the teacher and teaching assistant work together regularly, this might not be possible. Though it would be fabulous if all science teaching assistants were science specialists, this is unlikely to happen. I wanted to develop resources that the teacher and teaching assistant could use whether they have had time to plan together or not; whether they work together regularly or not; whether the teaching assistant is a subject specialist or not.

In some of the workshops I have run for teachers, teaching assistants and senior leaders, I have asked for the reasons that teaching assistants are often under used. The same sorts of issues arise time and again. I will explore each of these issues in turn.

Please bear in mind that it is by no means all doom and gloom. Some possible solutions to each of these issues will be proposed at the end of the chapter, but I think it is important to acknowledge the reality of where many teachers and teaching assistants find themselves as a start to the book. And also to acknowledge that those of you reading this book may not, at the moment, have a huge amount of influence on these issues. Bear in mind, though, that this is likely to change once teacher and teaching assistant start using together the strategies set out in this book. People will notice a buzz coming from your classroom that they will want to emulate, and you will be amazed at how you can influence the whole school by showing how it can be done.

High turnover of teaching assistants

There has been a significant increase in the number of teaching assistants employed by schools in the past ten years. However, many teaching assistants in secondary schools don't tend to remain as teaching assistants for very long. Some teaching assistants take the job because it fits in with the school holidays of their own children and move into other jobs when their children become teenagers. Some teaching assistants take on the role in a 'gap year' between school and university, or other work. The pay is fairly low and the demands of the role can be high. A particular stress can be the 'floating' nature of the role, where a teaching assistant may be working with five or more different teachers or departments in a day. This can be difficult because the teaching assistant has to move between lessons and adapt to the expectations and routines of different staff and pupils. Another reason for the high turnover is that many teaching assistants who find they have a flair for the role decide to progress into teaching; some of you reading this may be considering eventually training as a teacher. Recently, the option of becoming a higher level teaching assistant has become more widely available, and this may be an appropriate route for a limited number of teaching assistants in a school (for more about becoming accredited as a higher level teaching assistant see page 116). This leads me to the next issue that has been repeatedly raised as an issue for some teaching assistants…lack of continuity.

Lack of continuity

This issue of continuity goes to the heart of effective practice and may explain the finding that teachers in primary schools were more satisfied with the allocation of teaching assistant support than teachers in secondary schools (Smith *et al.,* 2004). In primary schools, teaching assistants are more often 'attached' to a teacher or a particular class. This allows the teacher, teaching assistant and pupils to establish solid relationships, with a good understanding of needs and expectations between them. In secondary schools, there are various models used, but the model of a teaching assistant 'attached' to a teacher is very uncommon. Common models of deployment include: teaching assistant 'attached' to a pupil and works with that pupil in the core subjects, but is used in different classes when that pupil has non-core classes; teaching assistant 'attached' to a year group and moves between classes according to need; teaching assistants assigned daily to different groups or individuals (this model tends to create the most challenge in terms of continuity, but is not uncommon). A final model, one that will be explored in depth in the next chapter, is that of the teaching assistant being attached to a department. This is a powerful model and one cited as 'good practice' by a recent National Foundation for Educational Research report (Wilson *et al.,* 2007). This model is also the one that is favoured by the Training and Development Agency (TDA).

Some schools are moving towards a model where teaching assistants are line managed by subject leaders or higher level teaching assistants. In other schools, teaching assistants are line managed by the special educational needs co-coordinator (SENCO). Some teachers and teaching assistants have identified that the degree of flexibility displayed by the line manager in a school has a huge impact on the way that teachers are able to use teaching assistants in that school.

A model repeatedly cited as a 'blocker' to effective use of a teaching assistant is if the teaching assistant is told to work only with the pupil to whom they have been 'allocated'. Of course, there are sometimes very good reasons for such an approach – when it is a 'blanket' demand, it can become problematic, particularly when one considers some of the evidence from research projects that have been carried out in this area. Tennant (2001) found that the presence of a teaching assistant could prevent class teachers from considering their own role in adapting the curriculum to ensure pupil access and participation. This is clearly undesirable, particularly given the evidence that teaching assistants often receive little training. Howes *et al.*, (2003), found that paid support staff can sometimes undermine inclusion by working in relative isolation with the pupils they are supporting and not helping 'their' pupils to engage with other pupils and the teacher. Research has also found that such an approach can lead to pupil dependence on adult support (Giangreco *et al.*, 1997). When group work approaches are used in mainstream classes with pupils with special educational needs, there is evidence of a positive impact on learning and participation. Group work also improves the pupils' views of their own competence, acceptance and self-worth (Nind *et al.*, 2004). It seems that group work might be a productive way forward. A variety of approaches that encourage group work are explored in chapter 4.

Another point made by a teaching assistant at a workshop on the effective use of teaching assistants was that teaching assistants are often not covered when they are absent, which seems to reflect the feeling that they are not really valued. Some teaching assistants have noted that the teacher of a class rarely comments upon their return after absence. Though perhaps understandable given the busyness and intensity of the teachers' role, this certainly does not help teaching assistants to feel that they are valued members of the team. Some Local Authorities have a pool of supply teaching assistants and higher level teaching assistants and encourage schools to use them to cover for known absences.

No time to meet and plan

No time to meet and plan is, of course, related to the point above. In a school where the teacher and teaching assistant don't know until they meet at the classroom door that they will be working together that lesson, it isn't surprising that the planning they are able to carry out is minimal or non-existent. This lack of time for teaching assistants and teachers to plan together and evaluate their work was also a finding of Cajkler *et al.*, (2007). But that does not mean that the teaching assistant can't be extremely effective at supporting the pupils in that class, it just means that the teacher and teaching assistant will not have time to plan their work together.

Teaching assistants not confident in pedagogy and the scientific knowledge and skills needed

The word pedagogy comes from Ancient Greek and literally translates as 'to lead the child'; it is about leading a young person through their learning. Pedagogy incorporates the variety of ways that learning can be structured and facilitated. It is about both natural ability and an effective application of strategies and ways of working that we know help people to learn. A teaching assistant, perhaps initially working with one, two or a few pupils, is in a position to have a profound effect on their learning, through the questions they ask, the strategies they select and the feedback they give.

You may feel that you know instinctively what you need to do and easily support the pupils to make excellent progress and develop their independence; you may just do your best to help them 'keep up' with the rest of the class and struggle to get the pupil to engage with the learning at all – I have met teaching assistants from both ends of the spectrum and most points in-between.

Knowing how to help

Having a good understanding of pedagogy can be likened to having a well-thumbed Haynes car manual at your disposal when you are trying to fix your car. Haynes manuals contain detailed diagrams and charts about how different makes and models of cars work, and instructions on how to fix things that might go wrong. In maintaining your car there will be straightforward things that are easy to address such as changing the oil, topping up the washer fluid and replacing faulty bulbs. These are simple to learn and, once you know how to do them, you can repeat the action when required with some success. You don't need to refer to the manual.

But what if the headlight bulb repeatedly blows? What if the oil seems to be running low much more frequently than expected? This is where your Haynes manual is most useful. The manual gives you detailed information on how the car works. You can look at the diagrams and work your way through them to make some educated guesses at what the problem might be. Perhaps the feeder pipe for the oil has a leak where it meets the engine block. You could check that and see whether there is a problem there. If not, you can continue to work your way back through the diagram to see where the problem lies. This is analogous to having a good understanding of the 'art or science of teaching'. Some of what being an effective teacher or teaching assistant is instinctive – but much of it can be learned.

Other findings of the literature review of Cajkler *et al.,* (2007) were that, though teaching assistants support learning under the direction of the teacher, they also work to some extent unsupported and often make decisions about the best teaching methods to use to address a particular area of difficulty with a pupil. Of course, sometimes the pupil will have a difficulty or misconception that the teaching assistant has not experienced. For teaching assistants who have had limited training, this can be likened to having a problem with a car that they haven't come across before; one that can't be solved with any of the strategies they have used before. Some teaching assistants may initially feel uncomfortable with this, particularly if they have received limited training. You can see how a Haynes manual (or the teaching equivalent) would come in useful here!

This book aims to give you the basics that will help you to understand the processes that pupils need to go through to come to a particular level of understanding, see chapter 3. This can be likened to the detailed diagrams in a car manual that show how the different parts of the car work and are linked together. When a pupil is 'stuck', a good understanding of this section will help you to identify where the problems might be and to develop strategies to help move the pupil on. Chapter 4 is rather like the 'step-by-step' instructions in a car manual that will help you to solve a particular problem that you have identified. If you enjoy this book and find it useful, I would also encourage you to read other books that develop an understanding of pedagogy; a great place to start is *The Teacher's Toolkit* by Paul Ginnis.

Teaching assistants may not feel confident in the subject knowledge and practical work skills that they feel they need to effectively support the learning in science. There are many strategies in this book that help to address this and many opportunities to 'skill up' in this area. Don't forget that there will almost certainly be areas where the teacher also feels less confident; these areas may be fertile ground for collaboration as you work together to lead the pupils through the learning. It is also worth bearing in mind that pupils view teaching assistants as role models of how to learn (Cajkler *et al.,* 2007). Never be afraid to admit you don't understand something – helping pupils to learn *how* to find something out is infinitely more valuable than giving them the answer.

This book has ideas that will boost the confidence of teaching assistants. The effective use of learning objectives (being clear about what pupils are expected to learn during a lesson), learning outcomes (the outcome that a pupil produces to demonstrate what they have learned; these can be leveled or graded to help pupils be aware of the standards they are aiming for) and success criteria (remember to... statements that help pupils to reach the learning outcomes) goes a long way to helping to address confidence issues. Where lessons are not learning-objective driven, pupils and teaching assistants do not know what is expected of them. This makes it extremely difficult to move pupils forward in their learning.

Misunderstanding of the particular issues a pupil faces

When teaching assistants have a good personal knowledge of the pupils they support it has a positive impact on pupils' learning (Howes *et al.,* 2003). It can be hard to gain a good understanding and relationship with pupils if the school model of teaching assistant deployment does not support this. Ways to help improve the model of deployment of teaching assistant in your school will be discussed further later in the book.

It is important to gather as much information about what pupils need to help them move their learning on from the SENCO, the teacher and the pupil. Teaching assistants report that they can often be seen as a 'mediator' between the pupil and the class teacher, and that teaching assistants can sometimes have a more positive relationship with pupils because they are not seen as such 'authority figures' as teaching staff. This experience of the teaching assistants interviewed reflects the findings of Cajkler *et al.,* (2007), who found that, in secondary schools, pupils perceived teaching assistants as co-learners and models of how to learn. Less positively, the same study found that some pupils, older pupils in particular, found interventions by teaching assistants could be intrusive and unhelpful. This reinforces the need for teaching assistants to have a good knowledge of the emotional and learning needs of the pupils with whom they work.

Lack of clarity over role

Support staff, teachers and, where appropriate, pupils, should work together in planning and implementing programmes of work (Howes *et al.,* 2003). However, the remit for a teaching assistant and the amount of input they should expect from the teacher is often not agreed between the teacher and the teaching assistant. This is not just a matter of expectations between the individuals concerned – it is also about the job description in its widest sense. This does not mean that the teaching assistant is without a job description; rather that the teacher does not see it, or that where the teacher is familiar with the teaching assistant's job description, the teacher and the teaching assistant do not have a good shared understanding of what it means. So, where the job description says 'To support the classroom teacher', the teaching assistant might be waiting for the teacher to tell him or her what to do with a pupil or small group, while the teacher expects that the teaching assistant should take the initiative and do what she or he thinks will be most helpful. After only a few lessons, the teacher may feel that the teaching assistant is not up to much, having not taken the initiative and supported the pupils, and the teaching assistant may feel unneeded or unwanted, having not been directed by the teacher.

An issue that can arise when the teaching assistant and teacher independently make assumptions about the role of the teaching assistant can be seen in the following example. A teaching assistant may be allocated to a pupil who, as well as specific learning difficulties, has poor behaviour in lessons. The teacher may assume that the teaching assistant will manage the pupil's behaviour, since they are sitting together. The teaching assistant may have made the assumption that she is there to support the learning of the pupil, and that behaviour management in the classroom is the sole domain of the teacher, so may wait for the teacher to reprimand the pupil for poor behaviour. In this way, in a busy classroom environment, misunderstandings can easily arise. Teachers may not be aware that a teaching assistant has achieved higher level teaching assistant status and can take on a wider range of tasks. Every opportunity should be taken to develop a shared vision for teaching assistant and teachers working together. This will be explored in chapter 2.

Summary of chapter 1

There has been a huge increase in the number of teaching assistants in the past ten years, but in some cases their impact has been limited by a number of factors.

- Teaching assistants receive fairly low pay and there is quite a high turnover of staff.

- Studies have found that teaching assistants often receive limited pedagogical and subject-specific training.

- Often, teaching assistants are not well directed by teaching staff, and teaching assistants and teachers rarely find time to plan and evaluate their work together.

- A better understanding of how pupils learn science, and strategies to help pupils address their 'sticking points', would help teaching assistants to be more effective.

The way a teaching assistant is deployed within the school has an impact on their effectiveness.

- The way a teaching assistant is deployed is often co-ordinated by special educational needs co-coordinator (SENCO).

- There can be a lack of clarity between the SENCO, the teacher and the teaching assistant over the exact role of the teaching assistant in the classroom.

- Where a teaching assistant is attached to a specific department, the support they are able to give pupils is more effective.

'The world is moving so fast these days that the one who says it can't be done is generally interrupted by someone doing it.'
                                                                    Elbert Hubbard

Chapter 2
Moving forward

Objectives

■ To outline a vision for a classroom where teachers and teaching assistants work together effectively to move learning on for pupils.

■ To discuss some characteristics of good practice within classes, departments and schools.

> There are classrooms where the teaching assistant and the teacher work together, where time is found to discuss pupil progress and plan the next steps. There are classrooms where teaching assistants have confidence that they know what is needed to move pupils on, and they can deploy a variety of strategies to do so. In these classrooms, the teaching assistant and the teacher work in tandem and as a team, each moving the learning on for learners in the class. Both of them have a clear view of the progress each learner will make and know how to work towards that goal. The presence of the teaching assistant in the classroom enhances the learning of every child there, not just children who have extra support.
>
> This isn't pie-in-the-sky; it really is happening. And where it does happen, the learning is transformed.
>
> This chapter explores some of the ways to transform the learning in the classrooms in which you work.

I have noticed that classrooms where teachers and teaching assistants work effectively together tend to share other characteristics too. They tend to be classrooms where relationships are valued, where the staff as well as the pupils feel safe to learn. This positive, supportive environment in the classroom or school is called a good 'climate for learning'. The climate for learning is influenced by the physical and emotional environment in the classroom, and is enormously influenced by the teacher's approach and expectations of the pupils. When the climate for learning is right, pupils are self-motivating because they are learning for themselves, not for an external reward. External rewards are important but, although pupils enjoy receiving them and teachers enjoy giving them, they are not the main reason that the pupils want to do well. In a classroom with a good climate for learning, all individuals feel valued, and pupils are encouraged to learn from each other, as well as from the teacher. In a classroom with a good climate for learning, pupils and teachers are not afraid to say they do not know – such an occasion is seen as an opportunity to move learning on.

In a good classroom environment, the relationships between teachers and teaching assistants can thrive. For a start, the teaching assistant may feel more comfortable asking questions, both of the teacher and of the pupils, when this is seen as an integral part of the learning process. In addition, although the pace can be fast and the quality of learning is often very high in these classrooms, the dependence on the teacher as the director of the learning who provides a lot of input and instruction from the front is often reduced because the pupils take more responsibility for their own learning. This may give the teacher and teaching assistant more time to collaborate and be flexible during the lesson, deciding what the most appropriate support for individuals and groups may be at any time. Classes with a good climate for learning tend to have confident teachers. Confident teachers may feel more comfortable with less conventional models of teaching, such as taking a small group of pupils who have been making slower progress while the teaching assistant supports the rest of the class. There are several strategies to support this way of working in chapter 4.

Progression

Progression is one of the most important concepts in education. It means learning experiences being steadily more challenging so that pupils are presented with opportunities to move to higher levels of knowledge and understanding. A year 8 lesson should not only be based on different concepts, but should engage pupils at a higher level than a year 7 lesson. Information on ages and stages in the United Kingdom can be found here: www.familylearning.org.uk/education_in_england.html

Progression in learning involves learners identifying where they are and where they want to be, and taking steps to get there. Milestones along the journey help learners to identify where they are and how to pick up the route for the next part of their journey.

A useful analogy to illustrate progression is that of climbing a mountain. When the climber begins to climb the mountain, the terrain in the foothills is fairly straightforward. As the climber proceeds further, the terrain may become more demanding. The further up the mountain the climber goes, the more challenging types of terrain she may encounter. The climber has to draw on skills developed or practised previously in order to continue the climb, and learn or practice new ones to apply later on.

Progression through science is similar to climbing. As the pupil moves through the science curriculum, the intellectual demand of the range and content increases and the skills that pupils need to have in understanding how science and scientists work become more advanced. The understanding of How Science Works and the skills that the pupil has learned at key stage 3 are applied to new situations and further developed in more intellectually demanding contexts at key stage 4. Progression is the understanding of how these skills and concepts are developed.

The framework for teaching secondary science, released to support the teaching of the new science curriculum from September 2008, gives the progression through learning for both the skills of science and the range and content that pupils are required to understand. The descriptions of the 'milestones' on the route will allow you and your learners to identify where they are and where they need to go next, and then plan a route to get there. More about progression is provided in chapter 3.

As discussed in chapter 1, there are all sorts of reasons why the work of a teaching assistant may not as effective as it could be. Many of the issues particular to the pupils' learning are explored in chapter 4, but these issues are certainly not the only blockers to effective practice by teaching assistants. Some teaching assistants quite understandably feel that they are not paid sufficiently for their work to extend much beyond the classroom door; planning time is often not included as part of the job package, and so teaching assistants find themselves planning what they will do to help the pupil as the teacher introduces the work to the class.

Now, in some cases, planning independently may work well – particularly if the teaching assistant has a very clear understanding of the progression in the skills of the subject and a good idea of where the content is going. For example, if the class is carrying out practical work, it may be quite clear what the teaching assistant needs to do to help a particular pupil or group of pupils to move their practical skills forward. And if teaching assistants are familiar with that practical then this may be fairly straightforward. Many of the sections of chapter 4 aim to arm teaching assistants with the skills to enable them move pupils on in group talk, research, scientific writing and scientific enquiry in any context.

In my conversations with teaching assistants and teachers where there is a real synergy, a sense of purpose, and success in the work that they do together to move learners along, common features arise again and again.

Teaching assistant working within a department

It is a lot easier for teaching assistants to be effective if they are familiar with the work of the department. The biggest thing a school can do to improve teaching assistant support is to have teaching assistants based within departments. This gives teaching assistants the opportunity to become more familiar with the teachers and the science, and gives the teachers the incentive to invest in the teaching assistants since they are working with them frequently.

A teaching assistant based in a science department has a huge advantage; over the first few months of work in the department, he is likely to encounter a large number of the common practical activities and scientific concepts that he will encounter repeatedly. This repetition and experience of the activity, perhaps with several different teachers, allows teaching assistants to become 'expert' and improve their understanding of how they can best support the pupils in their learning.

Teaching assistants that work across departments may find it more difficult to obtain the knowledge and skills to move learning on. Teaching assistants can support behaviour, reading and writing across several curriculum areas with relative ease, but may struggle with practical procedures, science knowledge and most importantly the progression in learning expected of pupils as they move through the science curriculum. Where teaching assistants work across departments, they may only encounter a particular practical or process once a year and have limited opportunities to develop their confidence and expertise, and their understanding of the continuity of the curriculum and skills being developed by the pupils. All of this becomes easier when a teaching assistant is designated as a 'science' teaching assistant working solely with the science staff in the science department.

Teaching assistants report that their base in the department has been invaluable when it comes to intervention for specific pupils or groups of pupils. They suggest that having a good understanding of the pupils and what is required to get a particular level (see chapter 3), informs everyday support, as well as more intensive support of the type that may be offered through a booster programme.

Effective intervention identifies what pupils need to move on and helps them to do so. It should be part of everyday teaching and learning.

'If you are doing all these things in the classroom, when it comes to KS3 intervention, you will get a better idea of the pupils who really need the help and who would benefit from the intervention because I know the pupils and what they need to do to move towards their target. Intervention is taking place throughout years 7, 8 and 9, not just in preparation for assessments.'

Science teaching assistant

When a teaching assistant is 'attached' to a department, he is likely to be 'invested in', that is invited to training events and departmental meetings, and perhaps sent on training courses that support the departmental development plan. Some departments have a regular slot in departmental meetings, or whole meetings set aside for sharing resources, good practice and ideas and these are readily shared between teachers, student teachers, technicians and teaching assistants. For example, in a department with a focus on developing literacy, the teaching assistant may be sent on a course that explores strategies to support literacy development within the department. The teaching assistant would then become responsible for disseminating this to the department during a session focusing on good practice. This model can be extremely powerful, not only because the teaching assistant becomes better informed about the issues and developments in the department, but also because it helps the teaching assistant to feel valued as a member of the team.

There are other advantages to having teaching assistants working within departments. When teaching assistants work within departments, teachers and teaching assistants are likely to form closer relationships. Over time, teachers will also develop their confidence in the teaching assistant and this can be communicated to the pupils. Pupils who always see the same teaching assistant in the science department are also more likely to feel confident in their abilities and this can increase engagement. Opportunities to develop a shared understanding of what is expected of the teaching assistant across the department can be exploited, to the benefit of teachers, teaching assistants, and most importantly, learners. Some teachers and teaching assistants working together in a department also reported that they shared evaluative feedback on lessons, with each being able to offer the other constructive feedback to develop their practice.

Part of the team

When teaching assistants feel part of the departmental 'team', they will tend to stay with the department during coffee and lunch times, and to develop a loyalty to the department, rather than to the teaching assistant team. It can reduce the 'them and us' mentality that exists in some schools between teaching assistants and the rest of the teaching staff. In this environment, there are also opportunities to share ideas or insights that cannot be planned for – they are often called 'water cooler' moments. These are the moments when good practice and good ideas can be shared and these opportunities often have extremely productive outcomes.

If the 'norm' in your school is not to have teaching assistants attached to departments, your Head of Department may need to discuss this with the Leadership Team. It is quite easy to plead that science is a special case in terms of having a teaching assistant linked to a department. There are two particular strands of argument that may be effective. One argument is that is can be an advantage to have teaching assistants in science who have a particular interest in the area or a science background. This is not, of course, essential, but it can help with an understanding of the concepts and ways of working that are particular to science. Secondly, and, I think, more powerfully, it is important that the teacher and the teaching assistant feel confident in the teaching assistant supporting pupils in practical activities in science. As has been discussed earlier, the opportunities for a teaching assistant based in a department to become really familiar with the common practical activities used at key stage 3 and 4 are much greater than for a 'floating' teaching assistant. This familiarity is a considerable advantage in enabling the teaching assistant to provide effective support; particularly if this support is to be spread more widely than just one or a few pupils.

Working with data

The effective use of data and an understanding of what the data is telling us is crucial to planning the next steps for each pupil. This use of data and the systems used to record, process and store data on pupil progress may be a part of the training of teaching assistants in your school. Often, it is not, and the use of data to inform the next steps in learning is not as widespread as we would wish. One of the standards for higher level teaching assistant is to contribute to maintaining and analysing records of pupils' progress. If you are not familiar with the way data is used in your school, ask to be included in some training.

Some teaching assistants have reported that carrying out the more mundane administrative data tasks has really helped them to develop their understanding of data. For example, in one school, the teaching assistant was asked to transfer some data for a class she supported into the SIMS system. This task helped to develop an understanding of levels and where pupils in the class were in their learning. It also meant that the teaching assistant knew where to go to get data on other classes and pupils she was supporting.

Developing a better understanding of 'levelness', 'gradeness' and progression will be explored in chapter 3.

Departmental characteristics that help

There are certain departmental characteristics that help support teaching assistants in doing an effective job. Many of these are obvious, but I mention them here nevertheless; they may provide a useful list for reflection by senior leaders or heads of department.

In schools where the teaching assistant has had a big impact and has been positively received by staff, attempts were made to place the teaching assistants in departments that matched their interests and background. However, teachers and teaching assistants also re-iterated that personality and approach is more important than experience. Specifically, departments would rather have an inexperienced teaching assistant with a 'can-do' attitude than a teaching assistant with three science A levels and no initiative.

Another feature that seemed to encourage the inclusion and acceptance of the teaching assistant as a valued member of the department was if there was a good mix of experience within the department. Some teaching assistants reported that trainee teachers such as PGCE (post-graduate certificate of education) and SCITT (school-based initial teacher training) students were often keen to share ideas and spend more time planning with teaching assistants than were established teaching staff. Perhaps this is in part due to the lower demand on these people in terms of the number of lessons taught per week. It may also be a reflection on the increased emphasis in teacher training of the importance of working with and managing other adults in the classroom, reflecting the increase in the number of teaching assistants in the past ten years.

Clarity in departmental expectations for behavioural rewards and consequences is also important. Pupils and teaching staff need to be very clear about the expectations of teaching assistants in terms of behaviour management. There is a clear link between teaching assistants who feel confident in their ability to manage and handle discipline issues and a clear departmental policy enabling the teaching assistant to issue sanctions and rewards in the same way as a teacher. Such a policy allows the teaching assistant to enforce the reasonable expectations of the department and be supportive of the teacher, and raises their status in the eyes of the pupils.

School characteristics that help

It is no secret that Leadership Teams in some schools are particularly good at gathering information and views from the staff and pupils 'on the front line' and acting upon it, where it is felt that a change would move the school forward. The

Leadership Team is responsive to good ideas and well thought-out suggestions. I call these schools 'listening schools'. Some schools are less good at this, and it can be more difficult to implement change in this environment.

A listening school that is open to ideas from all who have a stake in the school, from the lunchtime supervisors, parents, pupils, to the staff and governors. A listening school is supportive of professional development for all and ensures that such professional development fits in with the whole-school development plan and is shared with other staff in order to maximise impact.

A listening school is fertile ground for the growth of a more effective model of working for teachers and teaching assistants; but it is not essential. Even if the school in which you work is not a listening school, the Leadership Team will hear about the effective work that you are doing with your department and want to know more. It is said that actions speak louder than words, and you will make them listen by the action you are taking in your department and the changes that this action will bring about. You may need to be more proactive in your approach to the Leadership Team, and more persistent in your determination to share your good practice more widely, but you will be able to do it.

There is information and a range of ideas about how to spread good practice through your school in chapter 5.

Summary of chapter 2

A good climate for learning supports effective practice between teachers and teaching assistants.

- Create a physical environment that supports and encourages learning and shows pupils and staff that they are valued.

- Ensure that teachers and teaching assistants share high expectations for progress for all pupils.

- Secure an emotional environment where positive, supportive relationships can flourish; this is most supportive for learning.

Have a teaching assistant as part of the team.

- Include the departmental teaching assistant in meetings and training.

- Regularly provide opportunities to share good practice between teachers and teaching assistants.

- Encourage teachers and teaching assistants to the share data on individuals and classes.

- Ensure that departmental schemes of learning are accessible by teaching assistants, and encourage teaching assistants to add resources and ideas to the schemes of learning where appropriate.

Have clear, shared expectations.

- Have a clear whole-school policy on how teaching assistants and teachers are expected to work together to support learning and make sure everybody knows what it is.

- Use every opportunity to support the high status of the teaching assistant in the eyes of staff and pupils, and enable the teaching assistant to issue rewards and sanctions.

'The great thing in the world is not so much where we stand, as in what direction we are moving.'
Oliver Wendell Holmes

Chapter 3
Making it work in the classroom

Objectives

- To show that progression is at the heart of learning, and to help teachers and teaching assistants see how a clear understanding of progression can move learners forward.
- To use the Framework for secondary science to build capacity within teaching assistants to develop strategies and resources to move pupils on in science.
- To identify how data can be used to inform planning for progress.
- To provide resources that can be used by teachers or teaching assistants that develop an understanding of 'levelness' (KS3) and 'gradeness' (KS4).

In order to move learners on, you must understand where they are, where they should be heading, and how to get there. This seems simple, but is often overlooked by those in the teaching profession, as well as by teaching assistants and even the learners themselves. A really good understanding of progression in science is crucial to a learner making good progress, that is, pupils knowing where they are in their learning, knowing where they need to go, and knowing how to get there. Teaching assistants can be very effective in facilitating this process. That is what this chapter is all about.

Driving school

In order to appreciate the importance of knowing where pupils are in their learning, consider someone who is learning to drive.

Imagine a group of individuals, each of whom wants to pass the UK driving test. Their experiences of driving vary from complete novice to someone who has an overseas licence, but each needs to get a UK driving licence. Each individual books a series of lessons with the same instructor and begins to attend the lessons once per week. Let us consider in turn the approach of two driving instructors.

The initial lesson for each of the learners is always the same; the first instructor drives the learner to a quiet road and gives some basic instruction on how to start the car, how to change gear, where the indicators are and so on. The driving instructor delivers the same driving lesson to each of their learner drivers, believing that these are the basic skills that must be covered by all learner drivers, regardless of what they have done before – after all, the instructor cannot guarantee the quality of any instruction they have had before.

Subsequent lessons consist of the learner drivers driving the car on increasingly busy and more complex routes. The driving instructor believes that simply practising driving the car in different situations will provide the driver with the skills he or she needs. Lessons are not targeted to the particular learner's needs, but the driving instructor makes sure that each of the learner drivers has the opportunity to experience roundabouts, dual carriageways and different environments and road layouts – all the things, in fact, that they will be required to demonstrate competency at during the driving test.

Comments and feedback from the driving instructor about the driving are few, and not particularly helpful. Some comments state the obvious, such as 'Try not to crunch the gears', and some are instructional '4th gear now'. Neither builds capacity within the learner to identify how to improve their driving performance in the future. The driving instructor's favourite piece of feedback, given at the end of each lesson, is 'Make sure you practice!'.

Practice, the driving instructor believes, makes perfect.

The learner drivers do practice, some more than others. Several, while they are practising, make exactly the same mistakes that they make during the driving lessons, reinforcing them so the mistakes become habits.

After 20 driving lessons, which the instructor has determined is the number required to sufficiently experience all the situations that may arise in the driving test, the learner drivers are entered for their driving test. Over half fail their test. Some give up driving all together, having completely lost their confidence in their abilities. Some continue with the same driving instructor, and perhaps, after several tries, do manage to pass the test, though the more times they try; the more they believe that they are a poor driver. This belief may stay with them throughout their driving career.

Other learner drivers change their driving instructor.

Now let us consider a different approach to driving instruction.

During the first lesson, the second driving instructor asks the learner drivers about their previous driving experience; have they ever driven before? Why do they want to learn to drive? If they have some experience of driving, he asks about things they have mastered and things they would like to practice more. If they have had some experience of driving before, he asks them to take him for a drive, and carefully observes how they handle the car, reflecting on whether what he (the instructor) thinks matches the learner's assessment of his own skills. Any mismatch between the learner's perception and his actual skill level has the potential to be an important learning point, as the learner will have to 'unlearn' his incorrect habits and realise that new habits will need to be learned. The driving instructor will focus on the learner's areas of weakness, also allowing the learner to practice and refine the skills already mastered as an integral part of the lesson, even though the focus of the lesson is something different.

The instructor gives each learner driver two particular aspects of their driving to reflect on and practice for the following week. Aware that some of the learners are not able to practice between lessons, he also reminds the learner drivers at the start of the next lesson what the areas of focus were and why. And he rehearses with the learner driver what 'good' looks like in each of these areas.

This driving instructor builds the confidence of the learner drivers, noticing and commenting on areas where they are skilled, encouraging them to further improve on these areas with occasional hints and tips. If the learner becomes discouraged, the instructor reminds him of why he wanted to learn to drive to help restore his motivation.

Soon, the learners are ready for their driving test. Different learner drivers are ready for their test after different numbers of lessons, depending on what their prior experience was, how fast they learnt and how much they had to improve their skills before they were ready. The learner drivers approach their driving test with confidence, knowing that they have addressed their areas of weakness. They are aware of the areas they need to pay particular attention to during their driving test and subsequent driving, as these have been reflected on and practised during driving lessons. The learner driver knows what is required of them in order to get these areas right and pass the driving test.

The confidence they have built in their driving skills helps them to stay calm and manage even difficult and unfamiliar situations they encounter on the driving test with ease. Most of the drivers pass. If they fail, it is probably on an area they knew they were weak at; this is an area that requires further attention. They resolve to improve on this area for the next driving test, and they do so, and pass the test the next time.

Through their driving careers, these drivers are reflective and confident. Their experience of learning to drive has been a positive one, and they take the opportunity, where it arises, to further improve their driving skills.

You can see immediately how this applies in the classroom. When asked how they can improve, pupils frequently say 'listen better', 'work harder', or 'revise more'. This is the driving lesson equivalent to continuing with lessons generally 'practising', but not focusing on those areas that really need improvement. As a teaching assistant often has only one, two or a few pupils to work with, you can see that the opportunities to personalise the learning for the pupils are enormous. When pupils and staff identify and focus their attention on areas of weakness, progress for these pupils will be much more rapid.

Building on primary science

When pupils enter secondary school at age 11, something that is often neglected, at great detriment to the learner, is a consideration and appreciation of the science and skills they have already encountered and mastered in their primary education. This can be a particular issue in some schools, where a solid transition programme between primary and secondary schools is not in place. The most effective teachers and teaching assistants not only know what the pupils achieved in their KS2 SATs, but also have a very clear understanding of what is in the primary curriculum for science. This is then extended and built upon in the first years of secondary science.

For an overview of science at KS1 and 2, visit the Standards Site. http://www.standards.dfes.gov.uk

The Programme of Study for Science at KS2 can be found on the QCA site. http://curriculum.qca.org.uk

Primary science education tends to be very strong on scientific enquiry skills. Pupils are naturally curious and the approach to learning at primary school often lends itself to extended investigations that encourage the pupils to gather a range of evidence from several sources. Primary science often supports cross-curricular working.

Scientific enquiry at KS2 is divided into two main areas: Ideas and evidence in science and Investigative skills. The ideas and evidence section encourages pupils to generate their own evidence and also find evidence from other sources to test an idea. The area 'Investigative skills' is about pupils planning an approach and presenting data in suitable ways, as well as drawing conclusions and evaluating their work.

Primary science encompasses the same broad topic areas as science at KS3. As well as Sc1: Scientific enquiry, pupils study Sc2: Life processes and living things, Sc3: Materials and their properties and Sc4: Physical processes.

The tables that follow will help you to place pupils in the context of what they have learned before, and what is to follow, in order that you can build on their previous experience and knowledge.

This is a summary of the main areas of study taken from the Programme of Study for science for KS2.

	Topics	Sub-topics
Scientific enquiry Teachers should draw on the breadth of study in order to develop these skills	Ideas and evidence in science	
	Investigative skills	● Planning ● Obtaining and presenting evidence ● Considering evidence and evaluating
Life processes and living things	Life processes Humans and other animals	● Nutrition ● Circulation ● Movement ● Growth and reproduction ● Health
	Green plants	● Growth and nutrition ● Reproduction
	Variation and classification	
	Living things in their environment	● Adaptation ● Feeding relationships ● Microorganisms
Materials and their properties	Grouping and classifying materials Changing materials Separating mixtures of materials	
Physical processes	Electricity Forces and motion Light and sound	● Simple circuits ● Types of force ● Everyday effects of light ● Seeing ● Vibration and sound
	The Earth and beyond	● The Sun, Earth and moon ● Periodic changes

Extract from: The National Curriculum for England: Science

There are four attainment targets at KS2 (ATs): AT1 (Scientific enquiry), AT2 (Life processes and living things), AT3 (Materials and their properties) and AT4 (Physical processes). Pupil outcomes for these attainment targets at KS2 are measured using levels. What a pupil needs to do to achieve at each level is detailed in the attainment targets for KS2, which are found in the Programme of Study for KS2.

Pupils currently take Standard Assessment Tests (SATs) at the end of KS2 to determine the outcome of their learning in terms of the level they have reached. This is the level that is reported for science when they arrive in year 7 at secondary school.

Science at key stage 3

As at KS2, in KS3 there are four attainment targets (ATs): AT1 (How Science Works), AT2 (Organisms, their behaviour and the environment), AT3 (Materials, their properties and the Earth) and AT4 (Energy, forces and space). Pupil outcomes for these attainment targets at KS3 are again measured using levels. What a pupil needs to do to achieve at each level is detailed in the attainment targets for KS3, which are found in the Programme of Study. There is further discussion on this, and details of where to download the attainment targets from the Programme of Study for KS3, later in the chapter.

A summary of the main areas of study taken from the Programme of Study for science for KS3.

		Topics	Sub-topics
Key concepts and key processes		Key concepts	● Scientific thinking ● Applications and implications of science ● Cultural understanding ● Collaboration
		Key processes	● Practical and enquiry skills ● Critical understanding of evidence ● Communication
Range and content		Organisms, behaviour and health	● Life processes ● Human reproduction ● Diet, drugs and disease and their effects ● Variation ● Behaviour
		Chemical and material behaviour	● Particle model ● Elements and compounds ● Chemical patterns
		The environment, Earth and universe	● Geology ● Human activity and environmental change
		Energy, electricity and forces	● Astronomy and space science ● Properties of energy ● What forces are ● Effects of current in a circuit

Extract from:
The National
Curriculum for
England: Science

Science at key stage 4

At KS4, there are several different Awarding Bodies that offer GCSE science courses. All the Awarding Bodies have to use the Programme of Study for science at KS4 as their starting point for any science course. The GCSE course derived from the Awarding Body's interpretation of the Programme of Study has to be approved by QCA before it can be offered to pupils.

This is a summary (overleaf) of the main areas of study taken from the Programme of Study for Science for KS4.

The main area of study at KS4

How Science Works teachers should draw on the breadth of study in order to develop these	Topics	Sub-topics
	Data, evidence, theories	• Analysis and collection of data and explanations • Interpreting data and testing theories • Using scientific theories, models and ideas • There are some questions science cannot answer, and some. it cannot address
	Practical and enquiry skills	• Planning • Collecting data from primary and secondary sources • Working accurately and safely, alone and in groups • Evaluate data collection methods, considering validity and reliability
	Communication skills	• Recall, analyse, interpret, apply and question scientific ideas and information • Use qualitative and quantitative approaches • Present information, develop argument, draw conclusions, using appropriate scientific language and convention
	Applications and implications of science	• Contemporary scientific developments and their benefits, drawbacks and risks • Consider how and why decisions about science are made • How uncertainties about science change over time and the role of the scientific community
Breadth of study	Organisms, behaviour and health	• Adaptation • Variation • Genetics • Homeostasis • External influences on the body
	Chemical and material behaviour	• Atoms and their role in chemical change • Patterns in chemical reactions • Making new substances • Properties and functions of materials
	Energy, electricity and radiations	• Energy transfers and efficiency • Electrical power • Radiations and energy transfer • Waves and communication
	Environment, Earth	• Effect of human activity on the and universe environment and assessment of impact • Evolving atmosphere of the Earth • Changing universe

Extract from: Programme of Study KS4: Science

At KS4, student attainment is measured using grade descriptors, which are published by QCA and are the same for all Awarding Bodies. Outcomes are measured in grades. There is more about grades and grade descriptors later in the chapter.

The National Strategy has produced some extremely useful resources to support planning for progression and to help to structure learning through key stages 3 and 4. One such resource is the 'Framework for teaching science', which shows progression through years 7 to 11 in both How Science Works and Range and content. Each of the yearly learning objectives indicates appropriate expectations of pupils in years 7 to 11. This is to do with raising expectations for pupils; of course if a pupil in year 8 has moved beyond the expectations for year 8 then the progression to the next step in their learning is clearly indicated in the framework and should be taken.

The Framework can be found at: http://nationalstrategies.standards.dcsf.gov.uk/secondary/secondaryframeworks/scienceframework You can also download a copy of the Framework from this web page.

The Framework is divided into two main strands for both KS3 and KS4; How Science Works and Range and content.

Framework for secondary science

Strands	Substrands	Sub-substrands
How Science Works	1.1a Explanations, argument and decisions	1.1a1 Scientific thinking: developing explanations using ideas and models
		1.1a2 Scientific thinking: challenge and collaboration in the development of explanations
		1.1a3 Scientific thinking: developing argument
		1.1.1b Applications, implications and cultural understanding
		1.1.1c Communication for audience and with purpose
	2 Practical and enquiry skills	1.1.2a Using investigative approaches: planning an approach
		1.1.2b Using investigative approaches: selecting and managing variables
		1.1.2c Using investigative approaches: assessing risk and working safely
		1.1.2d Using investigative approaches: obtaining and presenting primary evidence
		1.1.2e Working critically with primary evidence
		1.1.2f Working critically with secondary evidence
Range and content	Organisms, behaviour and health	2.1 Life processes 2.2 Variation and interdependence 2.3 Behaviour
	Chemical and material behaviour	3.1 Particle models 3.2 Chemical reactions 3.3 Patterns in chemical reactions
	Energy, electricity and forces	4.1 Energy transfer and electricity 4.2 Forces
	The environment, Earth and the universe	5.1 Changing environment and sustainability 5.2 Changing Earth 5.3 Earth, space and beyond

Extract from: The National Strategies Secondary: The framework for secondary science: overview and learning objectives

How Science Works 1.1a3: Scientific thinking – developing argument

Year 7	Year 8	Year 9	Year 10	Year 11
Identify a range of scientific data and other evidence to back an argument and the counterclaim in familiar or simple contexts, e.g. establishing a wind farm	Identify a range of scientific data and other evidence to back an argument and the counterclaim in less familiar or more complex contexts, e.g. use of antibiotics	Use criteria to select relevant scientific data and other sources of evidence to support or negate an argument	Explain how the use of criteria improves the effectiveness of selecting scientific data and other sources of evidence to support or negate an argument	Devise criteria to select relevant scientific data and other sources of evidence to support or negate an argument in familiar contexts

Extract from: The National Strategies Secondary: The Framework for secondary science: overview and learning objectives

The great thing about the Yearly Learning Objectives in the Framework is that they show the progress that a pupil is expected to make through each strand. That means that, no matter what year the pupil is in, you can determine what their next step is, and give the pupil the opportunity to take that step. For example, in this extract from the Framework, the progression in the sub-substrand 'developing scientific argument' (1.1a3 in overview, above) is described.

Imagine you are working with pupils who are in year 10 and working on a case study where they are required to research a scientific question and create a reasoned argument for their point of view. One pupil is not currently able to demonstrate the year 10 objective – she cannot explain how criteria can improve the chances of selecting useful data – so you track back. Can she use criteria given to help her select evidence? If the answer is no, track back again to the year 8 objective. Continue to track back until the pupil is able to demonstrate that she is able to achieve the objective. Then build on that, in order to help the pupil make progress.

You must start where the pupil is - the framework allows you to do just that – to help the pupil make progress, even if she is working below what is expected for her year group. Let's take this a bit further, using the same framework strand – remember, this resource is available for every area of the science curriculum – you can use this resource and this approach for every pupil you support. Consider what sort of activities and support will help the pupil to move from one statement to the next, i.e. what are the strategies you need to put in place to support the pupil in making progress.

You have a pupil who can identify some arguments for and against some simple

Year 7	Year 8	Year 9	Year 10	Year 11
Identify a range of scientific data and other evidence to back an argument and the counterclaim in familiar or simple contexts, e.g. establishing a wind farm	Identify a range of scientific data and other evidence to back an argument and the counter-claim in less familiar or more complex contexts, e.g. use of antibiotics	Use criteria to select relevant scientific data and other sources of evidence to support or negate and argument	Explain how the use of criteria improves the effectiveness of selecting scientific data and other sources of evidence to support or negate an argument	Devise criteria to select relevant scientific data and other sources of evidence to support or negate an argument in familiar contexts

pupil is here

Extract from: The National Strategies Secondary: The Frame-work for secondary science: overview and learning objectives ideas, but you suspect that she is just repeating arguments that she has heard before, and is not actually considering the argument herself. This means that she is struggling to choose the sort of data and information that she needs to construct an argument in an unfamiliar context. What could you put in place to move this pupil (or group of pupils) forward?

Idea	Explanation
Someone else's shoes Identify a local, but unfamiliar issue (such as a proposal to build a new road). Ask the pupil what she thinks of the idea. Have a variety of different 'role cards'; present the pupil with the cards in turn and ask what she thinks of the proposal. The cards should have statements such as: **Local businessman:** **Thinks that the new road will bring more business to the village.** **Parent:** **Concerned that increased air pollution might make their child's asthma worse.** **Conservation officer:** **Wants to make sure that valuable habitat is not destroyed by the new road.** Ask the pupil to put herself in the shoes of the person on the card. Tell her she needs to share their point of view at a public meeting about the road. What sort of information would she need to make her argument in a meeting?	As the pupil starts to explore the sort of information she would need in each of these roles, start to use the word 'evidence' to help her understand the vocabulary. For example, the parent concerned about a child's asthma might want to find out information about air pollution and asthma. Ask the pupil where the parent might get this sort of evidence. Who might the parent call as a witness to give evidence to the meeting? Asking the pupil to 'role play' this sort of idea helps her understand that different people will come to different conclusions depending on their point of view, and also helps her to start to identify a range of sources of evidence.
Source shuffle Create a card sort or 'diamond nine' activity with a variety of sources of evidence on it. To carry out a diamond nine card-sort, ask the pupil to arrange the cards into a diamond shape. Ask the pupil firstly to describe what each source of evidence is. Then ask her to arrange the sources of evidence in order of 'trustworthiness', most trustworthy first, at the top of the diamond. The less trustworthy sources then form the middle rows of the diamond, with the least trustworthy at the bottom. Consider, is trustworthy the same as reliable?	This exercise serves two purposes – firstly, it draws attention to a variety of sources that the pupil might use for evidence (some more successfully than others!). Secondly, it will encourage discussion around reliability of evidence. For this reason, this activity is usefully done in pairs, so that pupils can have conversations that will move them on in their understanding. For example, if a mum is a doctor, her evidence on smoking and cancer might be considered more trustworthy (or reliable) than if a mum works in a newsagent. On the other hand, if the evidence being gathered is about the numbers of newspapers sold and recycled in the village, then the second mother would probably give the better evidence. These are the conversations you want the pupils to have. These are the conversations that will move them on to the next stage.

Source shuffle cards

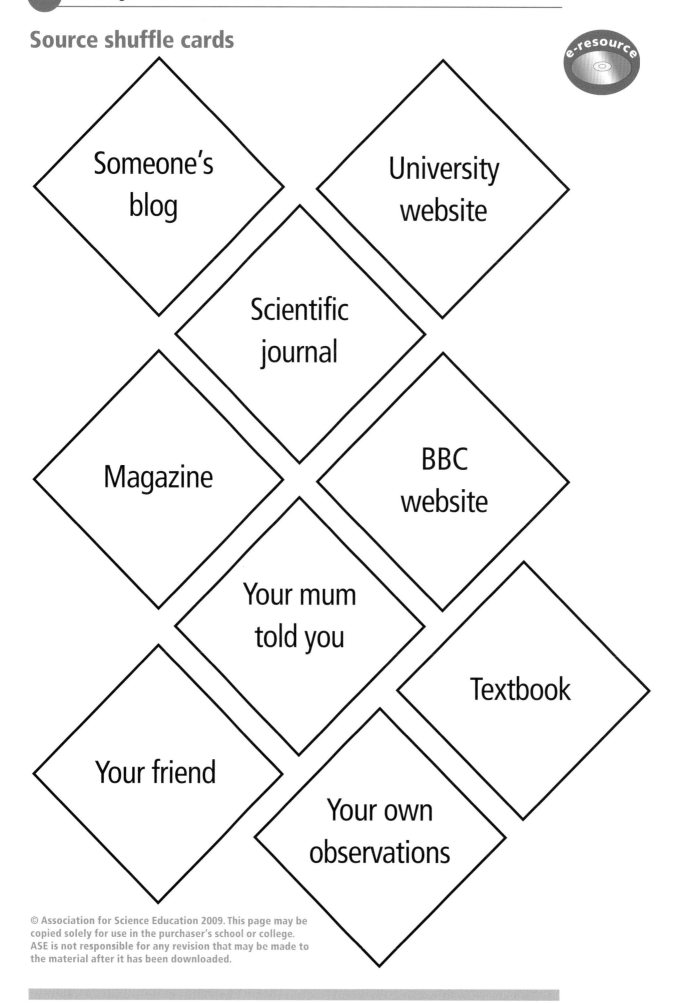

Let's take a look at the next step.

	Year 7	Year 8	Year 9	Year 10	Year 11
Extract from: The National Strategies Secondary: The Framework for secondary science: overview and learning objectives	Identify a range of scientific data and other evidence to back an argument and the counterclaim in familiar or simple contexts, e.g. establishing a wind farm	Identify a range of scientific data and other evidence to back an argument and the counterclaim in less familiar or more complex contexts, e.g. use of antibiotics	Use criteria to select relevant scientific data and other sources of evidence to support or negate and argument	Explain how the use of criteria improves the effectiveness of selecting scientific data and other sources of evidence to support or negate an argument	Devise criteria to select relevant scientific data and other sources of evidence to support or negate an argument in familiar contexts

pupil is here

In this case, we are trying to help pupils to understand the sort of criteria that would help them make good decisions about evidence. I am sure you get the idea. With a bit of imagination, you can create strategies in this way for each step in the progression. As you become familiar with the activities in chapter 4, you will see how they help to address some of these progressive steps for pupils.

Source shuffle (articulate)	One thing that might prove helpful would be to carry out the diamond nine source-shuffle, but this time pupils have to justify why they rated each source the way they did. You could ask pupils to articulate why they think a university website is more reliable than someone's blog, for example. They are using their own criteria when they make that decision. Can they work out and articulate what these criteria they are using are?
Criteria cards These have a series of statements on them, which may give an indication of the reliability of a piece of evidence. Pupils are asked to rate a piece of evidence using these cards. One way of doing this may be to use the cards from the source shuffle. Take the cards one at a time and put the criteria cards that apply next to it. The number of cards that you can put next to a piece of evidence from a source gives it a 'score' – the higher the score, the stronger the evidence.	Pupils will learn to understand what the statements on the cards mean and also pick up what scientists mean when they consider the evidence is reliable.

Criteria cards

The evidence has been reviewed by a group of experts	The evidence has been published by a professional organisation
The evidence has come from someone who has had special training in this area	Lots of people agree with this evidence
The people publishing the evidence are not biased	There is a good description of how the evidence was collected
The evidence has come from someone who has experience in this area	The evidence helps to answer the question I'm asking

How do you know where a pupil is?

As mentioned before, in KS2 (age 7 to11) and KS3 (age 11 to 14), in England, pupil progress is tracked using National Curriculum 'levels'. The progress of pupils who have not yet reached level 1 is tracked using P-Scales. Over 80% of pupils enter year 7 with a level 4 or 5, although some of the pupils you are supporting may well enter secondary school with levels lower than this. The levels are progressive; they build on one another. A detailed description of progression can be found in chapter 2.

Think of levels as similar to the grades that you can work towards when playing a musical instrument. You would start off with grade one; the pieces and exercises you are required to master to pass your grade one piano exam help you to develop the skills that are important for the grades beyond. The pieces you need to play are different for grades two and three, but so is the level of skill you need to demonstrate in playing those pieces. It is the same in science. The skills that pupils can demonstrate become increasingly advanced as they move through the levels.

It is important to note that in 2008 the KS3 Programme of Study for England changed. In the light of these changes to the KS3 Programme of Study, classroom practice is also changing to effectively support and deliver the science curriculum. In this chapter I have used the attainment targets from the new Programme of Study for science. These will be appropriate for use with pupils in year 7 from September 2008, pupils in year 8 from September 2009 and pupils in year 9 from September 2010.

Pupils finishing year 9 in 2009 or 2010 will continue to be assessed using the attainment targets from the previous Programme of Study, which can be found here: http://curriculum.qca.org.uk

It is important to understand what pupils at each level are capable of, so you can identify where they are and identify strategies that will move them forward. You can click through the site to find the level descriptors for the attainment targets on the QCA website: www.qca.org.uk Or go directly to the science page using the web address in the appendix.

From spring 2009, resources to assist in assessing pupil progress (APP) against the levels in the Programme of Study will be available. The APP assessment guidelines show exactly what outcomes are expected of pupils at levels 3–8. These resources encourage creative assessment of progress, allowing evidence of different types to be used to support the decision about what level the pupil is working at in that aspect of the science curriculum. The resources are also invaluable for developing an understanding of 'levelness', which will help you to be more aware of the activities that will help the pupils you are supporting to improve.

More information on assessment of progress is available from: http://www.standards.dcsf.gov.uk see appendix for details.

The level descriptors found in the Programme of Study are detailed in their expectations of pupils at different levels, both in terms of How Science Works (attainment target 1) and Range and content (attainment targets 2, 3 and 4). I have used the level descriptors for attainment targets 1, 2, 3 and 4 to produce a generic view of what is expected of pupils at each level, blending the way pupils understand How Science Works with the way they deal with Range and content. These are not a formal statement for assessing the progress of pupils; the intention is to create a tool that can be used in any context to help you get a better idea of what level a pupil is working at and how to move them on. The table describes what a pupil may be able to do at levels 2 to 6. These are the levels you are most likely to encounter in mainstream secondary schools.

After a while, you will start to get a feel for the level a pupil is working at without having to refer to the chart. This is an idea of 'levelness' and it is an

	Level 2	Level 3	Level 4	Level 5	Level 6
Scientific processes and phenomena	• Describe simple features of objects or organisms • Use simple features to sort things into groups	• Describe simple processes	• Describe some, drawing on scientific knowledge and understanding • Describe processes and phenomena, drawing on scientific knowledge and understanding	• Describe processes and phenomena, drawing on scientific knowledge and understanding	• Apply and use knowledge and understanding in unfamiliar contexts
Communicating ideas and terminology	• Use limited range of simple keywords • Use simple text, with help, to find information	• Use simple keywords • Use simple texts to find information • Provide simple explanations	• Use appropriate keywords • Make predictions • Select information from provided sources • Plot simple graphs	• Use appropriate terminology • Explain processes that have more than one step • Plot line graphs and bar charts	• Consistently use appropriate terminology • Take account of a number of factors in explanations
Evidence	• Respond to suggestions about how to find things out • Use simple equipment	• Can carry out a fair test, with help • Uses range of simple equipment • Suggest simple improvements to their work	• Recognise scientific ideas are based on evidence • Start to identify patterns in data	• Recognise that evidence and creative thinking contribute to the development of scientific ideas • Identify and describe patterns in graphs and charts	• Describe the evidence for some accepted scientific ideas • Identify, describe and explain patterns in data
Applications and implications of science			• Recognise some familiar applications of science	• Describe some of the applications and implications of science they are familiar with • Give examples of the applications of science	• Describe and give examples of the benefits and risks of less familiar applications and implications of science
Using abstract ideas, models and creativity				• Start to use abstract ideas and models in explanations	• Use a range of abstract models and ideas in explanations
Making links				• Begin to make links between ideas	• Identify links between topics and use these to write explanations of phenomena or scientific ideas

important factor in being able to move pupils on. For example, you will see that one of the differences between a pupil working at level 4 and level 5 is that a pupil at level 5 is beginning to use abstract models. There are several activities in chapter 4 that support pupils in developing their understanding of models and analogies in science. These activities would help a pupil at level 4 to make progress.

To make progress even faster, make sure pupils know what they need to do to make progress and give them plenty of opportunities to practice. The following 'pupil speak' resources may help you and the pupils you are working with to focus on what they need to do to improve. Strategies are suggested for levels 2 to 6. Levels 7, 8 and exceptional performance can also be gained at KS3.

The 'Strategies that will help' box refers to strategies in chapter 4.

Getting an idea of 'gradeness'

The Framework for teaching science gives an overview of the progress expected through key stages 3 and 4. The Framework can be used in the way outlined earlier in the chapter to inform you of the next steps for your pupils and enable you to track back or forwards if necessary.

In addition to the guidance from the Framework, it is useful to have an idea of what is expected of pupils at each grade. The following 'gradeness' guide should be viewed in a similar way to the 'levelness' guide earlier in this chapter: it is an interpretation and generalisation of the requirements at each grade and is designed so that it can be used in any context to help pupils move on.

At KS4 (years 10 and 11), pupils in different schools will study different exam specifications. The grade descriptors that tell teachers, examiners and pupils what they must be able to do in order to be awarded each grade are the same for all the specifications. That means, that with a bit of imagination, you can create a pupil-speak version of grade descriptors that shows what may be expected for each grade.

Please note that the published grade descriptors are only available for grades F, C and A – the grades in-between have been interpolated.

Students make faster progress when the standards required for each grade are linked to the learning outcomes.

I'm working at around level 2
To get to level 3, I need to…

- Know what the key words are and what they mean
- Start to read simple texts on my own to find answers
- Have my own ideas about how to do experiments, and choose equipment
- Be able to present information using graphs and tables
- Know how to use several pieces of science equipment
- Suggest improvements to my work

Strategies that will help
- ■ Equipment match-up
- ■ Focus on Progress in practical work
- ■ Scientific enquiry skill cards

I'm working at around level 3
To get to level 4, I need to…

- Talk about scientific processes and how they work
- Use what I already know as I begin to write explanations
- Know what the key science words are and use them appropriately
- Choose where to get information from to answer a question
- Start to make predictions about what I think will happen
- Choose the best way to present data
- Start to draw graphs, and to look for and talk about patterns in line graphs

Strategies that will help

- Focus on progress in practical work
- Sheep and eee's 94
- Scientific enquiry skill cards 66-70
- The hotel bell 99
- Research bookmarks 106-111

© Association for Science Education 2009. This page may be copied solely for use in the purchaser's school or college. ASE is not responsible for any revision that may be made to the material after it has been downloaded.

I'm working at around level 4
To get to level 5, I need to...

- Write explanations of what happens in a scientific process using what I already know and building on it
- Use the correct scientific words appropriately almost all the time
- Be able to draw bar charts and line graphs and know when to use each
- Be able to describe a pattern on a graph or in a results table, and suggest what the pattern is showing
- Use evidence from different sources to support an argument
- Explain how science is used in society, for example, how microbes are used to make some foods
- Start to use models in my explanations, including ones that are in my head

Strategies that will help
- The hotel bell
- Scientific enquiry skill cards
- Analogy cards
- Models and analogies stepladder
- The writing stepladder

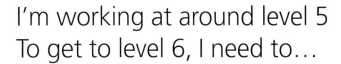

I'm working at around level 5
To get to level 6, I need to…

- Use what I know and what I've just learnt to write more detailed explanations of what happens in a scientific process
- Use the correct scientific words all the time
- Use what I know to work out what is happening in a new situation
- Think of several different things that could make a difference to the way that an experiment turns out
- Be able to talk about how some famous scientific discoveries were made
- Gather evidence from several suitable sources and present what I have found out appropriately
- Describe the good and bad things about the way some scientific developments are used (e.g. fertilisers)
- Be able to use several different models to explain things, and start to make up my own models
- Make links between different areas of science (for example, explain how the chemicals in fertilisers help plants to grow and also how this may affect food chains and habitats)

Strategies that will help
- The hotel bell
- Scientific enquiry skill cards
- Models and analogies stepladder
- The writing stepladder
- Research bookmarks
- Essay organiser

I am on target for an A grade at GCSE

I can

- Use what I know about how scientists work to plan how to answer a scientific question

- Use almost all the key scientific vocabulary accurately and appropriately

- Read questions carefully and write full answers relevant to the questions

- Apply the science I know to new situations

- Suggest improvements to methods and give reasons for them

- Draw and explain conclusions from data using detailed scientific knowledge

- Interpret data in the form of graphs, tables and charts, and also unfamiliar diagrams

- Give examples (including numbers that I have calculated using formulae, as well as taken from graphs, charts or tables) to support my answer

- Consistently choose the best way to present data and evidence

- Explain what is meant by reliability and validity, and apply my understanding when I carry out planning and evaluation of my own experiments, and those carried out by others

I am on target for a B grade at GCSE

I can

- Use what I know about how scientists work to plan how to answer a scientific question

- Use most of the key scientific vocabulary accurately and appropriately

- Read the questions carefully and write answers relevant to the questions

- Apply the science I know confidently in familiar situations

- Draw conclusions from data and explain them using scientific knowledge

- Interpret data in the form of graphs, tables and charts, and some unfamiliar diagrams

- Give examples (including numbers that I have taken from graphs, charts or tables) to support my answer

- Mostly choose the best way to present data and evidence

- Show that I understand what reliability is and I can demonstrate this by describing how to improve the reliability of an experimental method

I am on target for a C grade at GCSE

I can

- Use what I know about how scientists work to plan an experiment

- Use about half the scientific key words for the topic in my answers

- Apply the science I know to some situations

- Draw valid conclusions from data

- Interpret data in the form of graphs, tables and charts, and some familiar diagrams

- Spot patterns in data and describe the patterns

- Sometimes choose the best way to present data and evidence

- Give some examples of how to improve a scientific method

Using assessment and data to improve pupil progress

There is a crucial difference between gathering data on pupil progress and using it to inform the planning of teaching. Some assessment outcomes will be recorded as data, but day-to-day assessment is what teaching assistants and teachers carry out every lesson to determine where pupils are and what their next step will be. Assessment does have other purposes such as accountability and informing summative judgements on standards, but these are not really concerned with 'next steps'.

Day-to-day assessment takes place in every good lesson as the teacher and pupils make decisions about where they are in their learning. There are a number of ways to help pupils make decisions about where they are in their learning, such as clear learning objectives and outcomes, success criteria, effective plenaries, a positive climate for learning and effective feedback.

Periodic assessment takes place regularly, but not every day or even every week. In some schools, it takes the form of an end of topic test or similar activity, although some strategies encourage more diverse and creative ways of assessing pupils. An example is the Assessing Pupil Progress materials, referred to as APP, which will be available from spring 2009 to assist in assessing pupil progress against the levels in the Programme of Study.

The results of periodic assessment may be recorded by the teacher and entered into the school recording system, for example SIMS (Schools Information Management System) assessment manager. If this is *all* that is done with the assessment data, then this is not helpful for learning. It is the equivalent of the driving instructor saying to you at the end of a disappointing driving lesson – 'Well, you are rubbish at three point turns; will probably fail your test on those. Next lesson; roundabouts!'. APP will be a powerful way of helping pupils to move forward in their learning, helping you and them to identify next steps. It does, however, depend upon teachers having the flexibility to modify their teaching in response to what the data is saying.

In England in 2008, transitional assessment takes the form of teacher assessment at the age of 7, SATs at 11, and GCSE, or other, public examinations at the age of 16.

Assessment is powerful when it is used to inform learning. There are myriad ways of assessing where pupils are in their learning; some of these are explored in chapter 4. When you speak to pupils or listen to them talking in a group and you identify that some particular skill needs to be developed, make a record of this as something to work on in future. If a pupil persistently performs poorly on a particular sort of activity or question, then this is the area in which to focus your energies. Similarly, if the pupil is an expert in a particular area of the curriculum, then make sure the learning activities will be sufficiently challenging.

Data is also useful to inform you on where pupils are expected to be according to their KS3 or KS4 targets. Get this data from the teacher or from SIMS and ask how the targets are set. Increasingly, targets will be set to reflect the expectation that pupils will make two levels of progress in each key stage; that is to say, a pupil who enters with a level 3 from their KS2 SATs will normally be expected to achieve a level 5 at the end of KS3; a pupil who enters at level 5 is expected to leave with a level 7. This rate of progress is only possible where assessment is used consistently and intelligently to inform the pupil and teacher of the next steps in learning for that pupil.

Summary of chapter 3

Know where pupils are in their learning.

- Be aware of and build on what the pupil has encountered at KS2.

- Get a feeling for 'levelness' and 'gradeness'. This will help you to develop a better understanding of how to move pupils from one level to the next.

- Identify and use the strategies that best address the needs of the pupil and apply them.

Use the Framework for teaching science as your map of progression.

- Identify where learners are in the progression; only by knowing where they are can you take action to move them on.

- Use the Framework for teaching secondary science to inform you of the progression through the science curriculum, so you can back track where necessary.

- Be creative and devise activities that move the learners on – or use appropriate activities from this book.

Understand what assessment is really for.

- Assessment allows you and the learner to know where they are in their learning; this will help you to plan how to move on.

- Assessment takes place all the time and is powerful when it informs the next steps the learner should take.

- Summative assessment is not helpful for improving outcomes if it does not inform the next steps for the learner.

'When it comes to getting things done, we need fewer architects and more bricklayers.'

Colleen C Barratt

Chapter 4

Practical strategies that work

Objectives

■ To provide a range of practical strategies that a teaching assistant can use to support learning in the classroom.

We spent time in chapter 1 exploring some of the blockers to using teaching assistants to the greatest effect and in chapter 2, we identified some of the ways to overcome these blockers. In chapter 3, we developed a better understanding of progression in science, i.e., how to identify where pupils are and how to move them on. Now that you are familiar with effective ways of working, have an excellent understanding of the progression that is expected through science, and are able to identify where the pupil is in their learning, the next question is, What do you do about it?

The strategies in this chapter are a collection of resources that will help you to know 'what to do about it'. If this book was an éclair, this chapter would be the whipped cream in the middle; you can have the éclair without the cream but frankly, what would be the point? If you think of this book as a toolkit, chapters 1 and 2 are the training manual on how to use the tools effectively, chapter 3 tells you how to identify which tool to use for a particular job, and this chapter is about the tools.

There is a huge variety of tried and tested strategies to use with individuals, pairs, small or larger groups to help move learning on. So roll up your sleeves, and let's get going!

Problems and their solutions are on the following pages.

Section 4 *Developing writing*

Section 5 *An Intervention Programme*

Many learners struggle with group talk, this chapter will give you lots of ways to develop their skills.

Section 1: Developing scientific understanding

The problem

I'm not a science specialist and I feel out of my depth!

A solution

Focus on skills as well as knowledge

Not being a science specialist is often a concern for teaching assistants who are supporting students in science. If your school supports a way of working that allows you to work predominantly or totally within the science department, this issue will usually lessen over time, as you become more familiar and confident with the topics in the course. However, it is important to remember that information itself does not hold the same capital it once did. Less than a generation ago, pupils learned information from the teacher and also, sometimes, from textbooks, because that was where the 'knowledge' was. People were considered very clever because they 'knew a lot of stuff'. Exams tested learners on how much information they had managed to retain and awarded marks and grades accordingly.

The last few years in education have seen a radical turnaround in this way of thinking. The curriculum that came into force in September 2008 has, at its heart, a focus on creating successful learners, responsible citizens and confident individuals. This turnaround is not being driven by the curriculum; it is being driven by the way the world is changing. Information is now so freely available that most people are able to find anything that they need to know within minutes. It is no longer such an advantage to 'know a lot of stuff', because you can find out what you need to know so easily, and in fact become pretty expert in it fairly rapidly if you are skilled at interpreting and synthesising information. And that is the point; to be successful, pupils must know how to interpret the information that is so freely available. Universities repeatedly complain that students are not independent enough, don't have the skills to learn, and are not creative, and instead expect to be 'spoon-fed'. You can help support your pupils by helping them learn *how* to learn, not by always knowing the answers!

Skills that employers want

It really is worth reminding yourself that it is the skills outlined on page 47 that will really help your learners succeed. To be successful in supporting pupils, we must find ways to help them develop these skills.

Modelling study skills for pupils will help them improve.

Skill area	Specific skills	Person is / has
Self-reliance	Self-awareness Proactivity Willingness to learn Self-promotion Networking Planning action	purposeful, focused, self- belief, realistic resourceful, drive, self-reliant inquisitive, motivated, enthusiastic positive, persistent, ambitious initiator, relationship- builder, resourceful decision-maker, planner, able to prioritise
People	Team working Interpersonal skills Oral communication Leadership Customer orientation Foreign language	supportive, organised, co-ordinator, deliverer listener, adviser, co-operative, assertive communicator, presenter, influencer motivator, energetic, visionary friendly, caring, diplomatic specific language skills
General	Problem-solving flexibility Business acumen IT/computer literacy Numeracy Commitment	practical, logical, results orientated versatile, willing, multi-skilled entrepreneurial, competitive, risk taker office skills, keyboard skills, software packages, accurate, quick- thinker, methodical dedicated, trustworthy, conscientious
Specialist	Specific occupational skills Technical skills	specialist relevant knowledge, eg languages, IT e.g. journalism, engineering, accounting, sales

Source: Based on *The Art of Building Windmills: Career Tactics for the 21st Century*

If you want to develop your subject knowledge further, there are a number of ways forward. Asking the class teacher if you can borrow a textbook to flick through, so that you can stay ahead might be a confidence booster for you, and is easily done. The Framework for teaching science, published by the National Strategies is also an excellent source of information. As discussed in chapter 3, the Framework enables you to see how knowledge and skills develop over time; it has progression lines for each area of Range and Content and How Science Works, and will help you get a handle on where the pupils are and what their next step is to move on.

If you have a real interest and enthusiasm for the subject, most Tertiary Colleges offer Foundation or GCSE courses in Science that can be carried out in the evenings, and which your school may support. There are also many courses on offer that welcome both teachers and teaching assistants, for example those available through the Local Authority Consultancy support and the Science Learning Centres. If you wanted to train as a Higher Level Teaching Assistant, or develop your skills without training as an HLTA, your Local Authority may provide additional subject-specific training. There is more about this in chapter 5.

The problem

The student I'm working with doesn't know the names and the diagrams to use for simple science equipment!

The solution

Equipment match-up

Pupils who have not yet reached level 4 might struggle with the names and diagrams for basic science equipment. Here are a few ways to use the cards, see pages 45 and 46. I'm sure you can think of more.

1 Put all the cards on the desk and ask the pupil to see how quickly he can match the name to the diagram.

2 Put the picture cards in a pile in the middle of a small group and have pupils pick the card off the top. They have to name the equipment. If they get it wrong, or don't know, they are out. Winner is last pupil still 'in'.

3 As above, have a small group but this time they have to name the equipment and spell out loud or write the name. Winner is last pupil still 'in'.

4 When planning for a practical, ask the pupil to choose the names of the pieces of equipment he will need before he goes to get it.

5 When carrying out a practical activity, ask the pupil to match the diagram cards to the pieces of equipment.

6 When drawing scientific diagrams, have the cards handy for the pupil to refer to.

7 The pupil could have his own 'bank' of equipment cards and could add to it as he encounters a wider range of equipment

Card sorts can help to develop thinking skills.

Equipment cards 1

beaker	Bunsen burner	conical flask	heat resistant mat
test tube	syringe	thermometer	measuring cylinder (25 cm^3)
evaporating dish	filter funnel	clamp stand	measuring cylinder (100 cm^3)
tripod	gauze	round-bottomed flask	boiling tube

Equipment cards 2

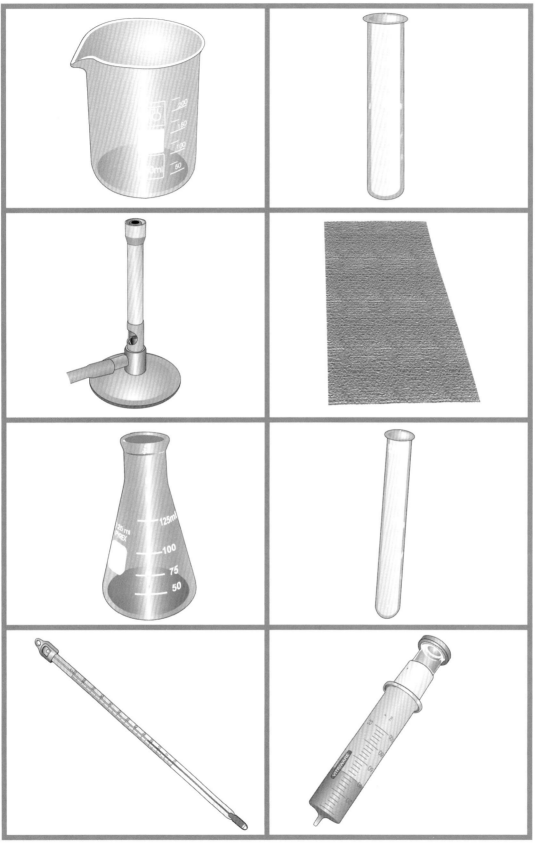

Equipment cards 3

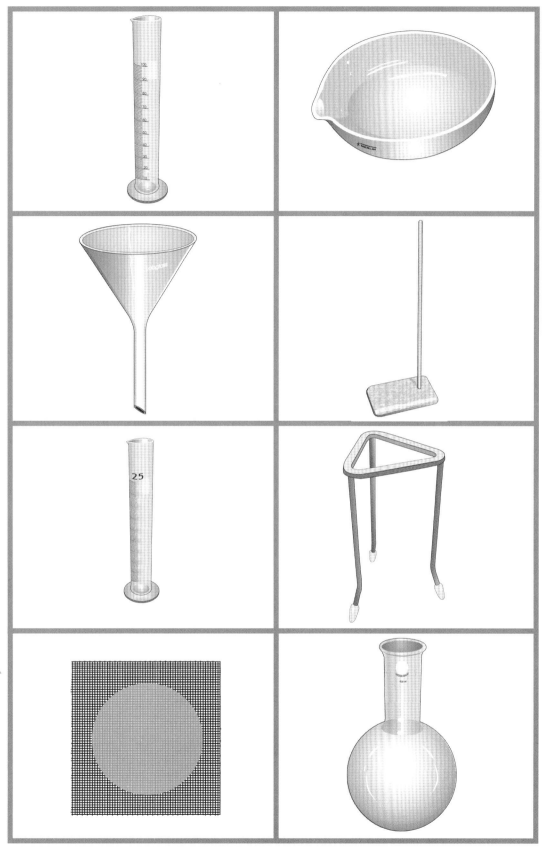

The problem

I don't feel confident supporting practical work.

A solution

Focus on progress in practical work

Sometimes you will be working with individuals or small groups of pupils who would find it difficult to access the practical without your help, perhaps due to mobility or behavioural issues. At other times, you might be called upon to help to support on a wider basis, circulating around the class to support the whole group, in conjunction with a teacher. At other times, you might be responsible for distributing resources. Let's take each of these scenarios in turn.

Working with individuals or small groups

It is important to remember that pupils are developing many skills when they carry out practical work in science. The yearly learning objectives in the National Strategies Framework for teaching science shows the progression in practical skills through the thread shown opposite.

This progression runs right through key stages 3 and 4. At the end of key stage 4 we would expect an able pupil to do what is detailed after the last arrow.

In supporting your pupils in developing their practical skills, it is likely that you will be working at the lower levels of the progression line. So what do the skills look like at the lower levels, and what sort of activities and questions will move pupils on?

These progression diagrams can be turned into placemats or printed out to put in the pupil's book or file. Use them as a focus to help the pupil develop the skills they need to work on at that time. Make sure other teaching assistants working with the pupil in science know what you are doing, so they can work on developing the same skill.

Obtaining and presenting primary evidence

Describe and record observations and evidence systematically

Explain how the observation and recording methods are appropriate to the task

Use and apply qualitative and quantitative methods to obtain and record sufficient data systematically

Explain how inherent **variation,** e.g. from human error, sensitivity and accuracy of instrument needs to be considered when collecting data

Use and apply **systematic** observation, **precise measuring** with a **range of apparatus** whilst taking account of inherent variation to obtain and record reliable data

Use and apply systematic observation, precise measuring with a range of apparatus whilst taking account of inherent variation to obtain and record reliable data in a **more demanding context**

Source: National Strategies Framework for teaching science

Progression diagrams

The pupil:
- wants to get 'hands on' but won't prepare a results table beforehand
- doesn't know what the practical is about but just wants to get going
- is more interested in the equipment than the outcome
- does not record results in a systematic way
- finds it hard to commit descriptions and observations to paper

Try...
- Let the pupil collect the equipment first so he can talk you through the method while showing you how he'll do it with the equipment
- Get the pupil to use a mini white board and marker pen to draw a results table – the pupil is much more likely to use it (who can resist a marker pen), and, in the initial stages of planning a results table, mistakes can be easily rectified.
- Ask the pupil to describe in words what is happening and then shorten it into the key words. These key words are what is written down. For example, if the pupil says 'It's gone all cloudy, I can't see through it now', ask him to pick the most important word to write in his results table. In this case, probably 'cloudy'.

Describe and record observations and evidence systematically

The pupil:
- can't explain why he is collecting the results he is
- answers 'to make it a fair test' to every question about the experiment
- doesn't suggest repeating readings.

Describe and record observations and evidence systematically

Try…
- Make sure pupils are very clear what question they are trying to answer with their experiment.
- Ask pupils to explain to you how the experiment will answer the question.
- Make sure the results table includes repeated readings, where appropriate, and ask the pupils to explain to you why repeat readings are important. Don't accept 'To make it a fair test' as an answer! Repeat readings don't make it a fair test, they increase the reliability of the results; that is, increase your confidence that if you did the experiment again you would get very similar results.

Explain how the observation and recording methods are appropriate to the task

The pupil:
• can record results in a results table, but is inconsistent with units or how many decimal places the results are being recorded to
• can explain why readings are repeated but is not sure how to calculate an average value
• is not confident when measuring with precise equipment, for example vernier callipers or syringes.

Explain how the observation and recording methods are appropriate to the task

Try…
• Help pupils to spot anomalies in their results and talk to them about what should be done about these anomalies.
• Show pupils how to calculate averages (or ask another student to show them), and talk about the different types of average they have come across in maths.
• Give pupils as much 'hands on' experience as possible manipulating the apparatus. This will help them to stay motivated as well as developing their skills.

Use and apply qualitative and quantitative methods to obtain and record sufficient data systematically

The problem

I don't feel confident in supporting whole class practical work

A solution

Start-up cubes

If you are circulating to support the whole class in a practical activity, it is important that you feel confident in the activity and have had the chance to have a practice go. As a vital part of the science team, lab technicians are a mine of information, and will probably be happy to help with information and advice. The technicians will be able to tell you in advance when a practical is scheduled for a lesson you are supporting and what the practical is. They will be able to show you how the practical works and let you have a practice run. During and after the practical you can help to make sure it runs smoothly and is cleared away appropriately by the pupils at the end.

If you are unable to prepare because of last-minute timetabling or a last-minute practical, you will be in the in the uncomfortable (but common) situation of finding out what the practical work is at the same time as the pupils. Listen carefully and do not be afraid to ask the teacher for clarification – after all, if *you* have not got a clear understanding of what pupils are trying to find out and why, then the pupils probably have not either!

Make sure you always model good practice by wearing a lab coat, having long hair tied back and wearing eye protection where appropriate. If you support full time in the science department, then it is appropriate that you have your own lab coat in the Prep room, which you can use whenever the need arises. Apart from helping you to look the part, it will also give you added confidence (and keep your clothes protected!).

Once the class has carried out the practical work, it is likely that they will do some kind of write-up. If you are supporting during this, it is a good idea to have some questions in mind to 'open up' the conversation. One way to do this is to use the Foam Cube as a prop to help you start up conversations with the pupils. Examples of what might go on each face are found overleaf, and additional detail can be found in the section about supporting coursework and case studies. Foam Cubes (called Giant Pocket Dice) can be purchased from www.craftpacks.co.uk

For each set of cards (there are six cards per cube), there is a detailed version with questions to ask, for you to start off with. In the electronic resources, there is also a version with just the titles, to use when you feel more confident about what the terms mean.

Using the start up cubes gives a focus for conversations.

Planning cube

Repeat

How many times do you think you should repeat the experiment?
Why do we do repeat readings?
(NB It is NOT to make it a fair test!)
What does reliable mean?

Recording

Does your results table have clear headings?
Does your results table have units?
How are you making sure your recording is accurate?
What are the possible errors in your recording?

Calculations

Have you carried out any calculations?
Have you written down the equation you used?
Have you specified the units?
Have you marked clearly what is raw data and what data has been processed?

Range

What range do you think the results will be in? Give an estimate.
What units will you be measuring in?
In order to get a good set of results, what are the highest and lowest values of the variables you'll be testing?
Have you mentioned the range of values in your planning?

Units

What units are you measuring in?
If you are measuring time, what units are you measuring in?
Have you included the units on your results table?
Have you included units on the axes of any graphs you've drawn?

Equipment

Is all the equipment working properly?
Is the equipment set up safely?
Are you using the most accurate equipment to measure that is available? (Hint: Equipment that goes to more decimal places gives you a more accurate result)

Analysis and graph work cube

Confidence

Do you think your results are correct? How much confidence do you have in them?

Do your results fit nicely onto a straight line or a curve?

The more the points fit neatly on the line of best fit, the more confidence you can have in your results – how confident are you?

Is there a pattern in your results?

Do all the results fit the pattern?

Calculations

In order to get the highest marks, you need to 'process' your results; this means carry out calculations on them. Examples of the sort of calculations you might do include averages, gradients, and working out pressure when you have measured force and area.

Have you carried out calculations on your results? What have you done?

If you have carried out calculations, what is the formula you have used?

Have you remembered to include the formula on the table where you have carried out the calculations?

Scale

Have you chosen the most appropriate scale for your graph?

Does the graph fill most of the graph paper?

Do your axes both start at zero? If not, have you shown this using a zig-zag line?

Have you included units on each scale?

Have you included enough sub-divisions on the scale?

Have you made sure all the sub-divisions are the same distance apart?

Best fit

Have you drawn a line or curve of best fit?

Is it in the best place? Why?

What does a line of best fit mean?

Make some predictions about results you didn't measure.

What is the relationship between one variable and the other?

Anomalies

Anomalies (or outliers) are points that don't fit with the general pattern, or don't fit onto the line of best fit.

Are there any anomalies on your graph?

If there are anomalies, try to explain them. How might they have happened?

To increase the amount of confidence you have in your results, repeat the results that are anomalous. Did you get a more sensible result the next time?

Pattern

What is the relationship shown on the graph?

(Hint: As one gets higher, the other......; as one increases, the other ....)

Conclusions and evaluations cube

Data

Have you referred to your data in your conclusions?
Are there any especially interesting results? Why are they interesting?
What is the range of your data? Is it what you expected?

Bias

Bias can occur in a set of data when you have an expectation of what the answer is before you begin. Do you think any bias has crept into your data?
How did you make sure your results and recording methods did not create biased results?

Reliability

When you repeat your readings, if the results are reliable, the values will all be very similar to one another.
You cannot tell whether your results are reliable if you haven't repeated any readings. Can you tell if your results were reliable?
How could you have been more certain that your experiment was giving reliable results?

Accuracy

Accuracy is to do with how close to the real value for what you are measuring you can get. For example, if you are measuring 6 mm and using a ruler marked in cm, your measurement will not be accurate.
How did you make sure your results were accurate?
How did you choose measuring equipment that would ensure accuracy?

Evidence

You have drawn a conclusion from your experiment. What information or data have you used to support your conclusion?
Have you remembered to give some examples of results to illustrate your findings?

Validity

If your experiment is valid, you will have gathered results that answer the question you originally asked.
Was your experiment valid?
Explain why.

A solution

Practical sheet mark-up

Often, a practical activity will come with a sheet of instructions for the pupils to follow. This may be displayed on the board, talked through with the pupils or distributed to the class prior to the practical. Practical activities are repeated often, across year groups in different classes and with different teachers, so you will probably have good opportunities to develop your skills and knowledge as you repeatedly support different pupils through the same practical activity.

There are many ways in which the practical instruction sheets can be helpful to you, so hang on to the practical instruction sheets. Here are some of the ways they can be useful.

● Take the sheet to the teacher and ask which parts pupils are most likely to need help with, and how you could help the pupils at that point. Mark this up on the practical sheet.

● Have a practice go setting up the apparatus and make notes on the sheet if there are any particular parts that might cause the pupils to have problems.

● During and after the practical, make notes on the sheet about any particular tips you would like to remember for next time.

● Think of good questions to ask at different stages of the practical and jot these down. Open questions (where the pupil needs to give an extended response) are more useful than closed questions, because they help pupils to develop their thinking and can reveal misconceptions. For example, asking 'What are the reasons for changing from an orange to a blue Bunsen flame when you're heating something?' is more useful than 'What is the black stuff the orange flame leaves on the beaker?'.

● Keep a file of the practical sheets and pull the sheet out of the folder the next time the same practical comes up. You will be amazed how much you know!

The problem

I want to be able to explain things in alternative ways to students and I don't know how

A solution

Allow yourself to be creative!

Okay, this is where you need to get creative. Using models and analogies is not by any means restricted to science. We use them all the time to make it clearer what we are trying to express. For example, when we would really, really like a cup of tea, we might say 'I'm parched'. Saying 'I'm parched' implies more than just saying 'I'd like a cup of tea'. The implication is that every cell of your body is crying out for an infusion of the magical golden liquid; that your tongue is cracked and dry from a lack of tea and that when tea is forthcoming, your internal organs will burst forth in flower with the sheer joy of the rehydration.

Or here's another example. 'When I told her the good news, her face lit up like a Christmas tree'. We know exactly what the speaker means. The implication is that the girl's face sparkled with joy, that she was transported with delight at the fantastic piece of news she had received.

You see what I mean. When we use a model or analogy to make our point, we can get a lot of information across in quite an easy way. It is a sort of conversational shorthand and it is extremely useful. Analogies are also a great way to explore ideas. When I was carrying out some development work with a teacher recently, we were discussing the work that we had done together. I proposed two analogies for the work; one was that he was on a long walk. Every so often I would appear and add a brick to his backpack. The brick was the idea that I was sharing with him. He then had to add that 'idea' to what he was already doing and 'carry' it; the implication being, of course, that each new idea amounted to more work. The alternative analogy (and the one that he agreed was more appropriate, I'm pleased to say!) was that his teaching was a car, and each new idea was a part for the car that would replace an existing part and help the engine to run more smoothly or efficiently.

Adults use analogies all the time, and they are extremely useful in science, as they help to deepen understanding and reveal misconceptions.

Examples of analogies used in science are 'a cell is like a factory' and 'an electrical circuit is like a central heating system'. The learning comes when the pupil is asked to explore the analogy further and explain why the analogy is true, and when and why it breaks down.

Let's explore the analogy 'a cell is like a factory' see opposite, so you can see what I mean.

You can see that a basic understanding of the cell and of the factory is needed in order to successfully explore this analogy. For lower level pupils, it would be useful to use a simple diagram of a factory and a cell where the processes that are going on in each are more easily seen and can be compared. Now, some analogies are more useful than others. The second example of an analogy given above, 'An electrical circuit is like a central heating system', is less useful, (although it is still commonly used in schools!). Can you spot why it is less useful? You've got it – most pupils (and also many adults in my experience) don't really know how a central heating system works, so they are not able to examine the parts of it in turn and see how it might be similar to a circuit.

The real strength of analogies and models emerges when the pupil begins to come up with their own. Pupils' analogies will show you the level of understanding they have and help you to clear up any misconceptions. For example, a pupil might describe particles of a gas as 'Like ping pong balls in a bucket'. You can ask lots of questions about the idea, particularly asking what are the strengths and weaknesses of it as a model or analogy.

Returning to the main 'Problem' of this section; having alternative ways to explain things. Do not be afraid to launch into an analogy. If you are trying to explain how something happens, think of a memorable and relevant everyday situation that will help the pupil understand and then ask them questions about it. In chemistry, a displacement reaction is one in which a metal displaces a less reactive metal to form a new salt. Pupils can find this difficult to understand at first, but soon get the hang of it if you explain it in terms of the 'displacement disco'. At the displacement disco, the most attractive and appealing 'partners' are those that are most reactive. Even couples that have arrived at the disco together can be split up by the arrival of one of these more reactive and attractive 'partners', who will then form a couple together, leaving the less reactive partner on their own. There are some excellent role play opportunities here, too!

The more science you are exposed to, the more of these analogies will pop into your mind. Once you become attuned to them, you will hear them used all the time. To get more ideas, check the internet. There are lots of websites that give examples of analogies that are commonly used in science.

A cell is like a factory. Why?

1 A factory usually makes something. A cell can make something. Cells make proteins in the form of enzymes to be used in the body.

2 Factories use energy. Cells use energy that they release in respiration.

3 Factories have someone in charge who controls what goes on and the manufacturing process. Cells have a nucleus, which can control what goes on in the cell.

4 Factories have raw materials that go into the factory and get made into the products. Cells use raw materials (for example, the raw materials for respiration or photosynthesis) and they produce products.

5 Factories have storage bays where the products can be stored before being collected and delivered to where they are needed. Some cells have storage areas (for example, the vacuole in plant cells where the cell sap is stored) to store products until they are needed.

A solution

Analogy cards

The analogy cards, see opposite, are a simple matching game to help pupils to build up their confidence in using models and analogies.

1 Pupils match the model or analogy to the reasons why it 'works'.

2 For each group of three cards, ask pupils to come up with another reason why the analogy 'works'.

3 Ask pupils to think of a problem with the analogy.

Models and analogies help learners to explore their ideas and understanding of science, and can help the teacher or teaching assistant to spot misconceptions.

Analogy cards

The brain	**The manager of a company**	**All the decisions are made and controlled from here.**
A car battery	**A lump of cheese**	**They both contain a form of energy that can be converted into another kind of energy.**
A human eye	**A camera**	**Both have a lens that focuses the image and a hole that can vary in size to let the correct amount of light through.**
Red blood cell	**Truck**	**They take things from one place to another, where they drop one thing off and pick another thing up.**

A solution

The models and analogies stepladder

Of course, using a model or analogy is only the first step. Pupils can improve the way that they use models and analogies. This stepladder shows how a pupil's understanding of models and analogies can develop. It may also be useful for you to use to develop your own understanding of models and analogies. It might also be useful to keep a note of when models and analogies are used by teachers and pupils in the lessons where you are working – you will soon have quite a repertoire.

Ways to move the pupil on...

The pupil is starting out using models and analogies

- She can see how something in science is like something else. For example, lungs are like balloons.
- She can explain why some analogies work. For example, lungs are like balloons because they can inflate and deflate.

- **Play the analogy game with the pupil.**
- **Pick two random things (for example, a window and a cup of tea), and ask the pupil to explain how they are alike using ideas about science. It can help to choose one area of science to use as the focus, like forces, particles, interdependence, cells or energy.**
  - **When you come across ideas in science, keep asking the pupil what it is like (a model for the system) and ask her to test the analogy on other people to see whether their ideas fit in with the science.**

**Ways to move
the pupil on...**

**I'm improving at using models
and analogies**

• The pupil can make up her own simple
models to explain what she sees, her
ideas or data she has gathered.
• The pupil knows that different models
are used in science to explain the same
thing.

• **When pupils are introduced to a new
scientific idea, ask them to try to suggest
a model that might be used to explain it.**
• **When the teacher or another student
mentions a model for a system, ask the
pupil you are supporting to think
about the model and how well it
explains the system.**
• **Ask the pupil questions about the
model to help clarify what all the parts
of the model represent.**

Ways to move the pupil on...

I'm taking using models and analogies further

• The pupil can identify and discuss the strengths and weaknesses of some analogies and models.
• The pupil can be creative in thinking of her own models and talking about the model with others.

• **When you give the pupil a model, ask her to describe which parts of the model represent which bits of the scientific system you are looking at.**
  • **Ask the pupil to tell you where the model works, and where it doesn't work.**
    • **Ask the pupil to think of ways that a model could be improved.**
      • **Encourage the pupil to explain to someone else how a model can be improved.**
• **Allow yourself and the pupil to have and discuss your own ideas in science!**

Ways to move the pupil on...

I'm skilled and confident at using models and analogies

• The pupil can choose an appropriate model to explain observations, ideas or data.
• The pupil can explain why the model she has chosen is the most appropriate.
• The pupil can be creative and think of her own model for a situation and explain it.

• When given a selection of models of a system, ask the pupil to identify the strengths and weaknesses of the model and use this analysis to choose the best model for the system.

• Ask the pupil to explain to friends and to the teacher why she has chosen a particular model.

• Ask the pupil to make up her own models and identify their strengths and weaknesses.

• Ask the pupil to talk about her models to other people, and improve the model if possible.

• The pupil can explain how and why the model has been improved.

Source: The progression in group talk activity was developed from an original idea by the National Strategies: Progressing to level 6 and beyond.

Section 2: Developing analysis and interpretation

The problem

I want to help pupils develop their analysis and interpretation of primary and secondary evidence

A solution

Scientific enquiry skill cards

It is no coincidence that some of the questions pupils have the most trouble with are those that ask them to interpret evidence, particularly secondary evidence. Typically, pupils might carry out an experiment, record the results, draw a graph and then be asked to draw a conclusion about the pattern on the graph. Pupils can generally manage to draw a simple conclusion when prompted, particularly if the experiment is still fresh in their mind. However, an equally important skill, and one that is not so well addressed by pupils, is the interpretation of data from an experiment that they themselves did not carry out.

The reasons behind this are clear; pupils find it hard to visualise what others have done in an experiment, and they often skip over the explanatory text and go straight to the question they are being asked. This needs to be overcome if pupils are to fully understand the nature of the science carried out by others as well as by themselves.

The skill cards first encourage pupils to interpret their own data, an important first step, and then progress onto the interpretation and evaluation of the data of others. The skill cards can be printed out for each pupil's file or book, or made into laminated cards for the pupils to refer to when they are analysing primary or secondary data. The cards are designed to be printed and then stuck back-to-back. Identify with the pupil which card is appropriate using the front, and then help them to make progress using the ideas on the back.

These cards would also be helpful for students in year 10 and 11 carrying out the 21st Century Science data analysis task.

Pupils often need help in interpreting evidence.

Scientific enquiry skill cards

Card 1 - Is this you?

- **I need help to learn to draw line graphs.**
- **I need practice talking through what the line on a graph shows.**
- **I need practice using the practical equipment, especially using measuring cylinders, electronic scales and rulers accurately.**
- **I need to practice working out what evidence shows me and drawing conclusions.**

These things will help you improve

- Ask someone to tell you what they are doing when they are drawing a line graph. They should give a commentary as they go, explaining to you what they are thinking as they decide a scale, draw and label the axes, put the points on and then draw a line of best fit, if the graph needs one.
- Every time you work with a graph, talk through what it shows with someone else.
- Practice measuring things out using equipment at school, using measuring cylinders and electronic scales, and also at home, using scales and measuring jugs.
- Make sure you know what the words 'evidence' and 'conclusion' mean – try putting the words into sentences.

Card 2 - Is this you?

- **I can draw line graphs, but sometimes I find it hard to get the scale right.**
- **If someone helps me, I can explain what the shape of the graph shows.**
- **In practical work, I am mostly confident at using the equipment.**
- **I can make a simple plan for a practical.**
- **I can choose which measuring instruments to use for a practical.**
- **I can draw conclusions that match with the evidence I have collected.**
- **I can look at someone else's evidence and draw a conclusion.**
- **I can sometimes spot patterns in data.**

These things will help you improve

- Ask someone to tell you what they are doing when they are drawing a line graph. They should give a commentary as they go, explaining to you what they are thinking as they decide a scale, draw and label the axes, put the points on and then draw a line of best fit, if the graph needs one.
- Practice talking through the 'story of the line' on pre-drawn graphs.
- **Practice describing the pattern on a graph** by using 'Er, er' statements (e.g. the high**er** the temperature, the quick**er** the melting).
- When planning, **think** about the plan, then **talk** someone else through it, and only then **write** it down.
- Make sure you know the **names and spellings** for common pieces of science equipment (e.g. measuring cylinder, Bunsen burner, beaker, tripod, gauze, test tube).

Scientific enquiry skill cards

Card 3 – Is this you?

- I can choose scales for graphs that show the data clearly.
- I can explain what the shape of a graph represents.
- I understand graphs with negative scales.
- I can draw conclusions based on evidence and use science to explain my conclusions.
- I know what dependent and independent variables are and I can identify them in experiments.
- I can choose appropriate ranges for variables in my experiments.
- I know that I need to make several measurements to increase the reliability of my results.
- I can measure precisely, using several different measuring instruments.
- With some help, I can carry out data analysis that involves calculations.

These things will help you improve

- Break line **graphs into sections** and see if you can describe each section separately, then put them together to tell the story of the line.
- **Practice drawing graphs** with appropriate scales, including negative scales.
- Make sure you understand what a **line of best fit** is and how to draw one.
- Look for and talk about patterns in data and graphs.
- Remember that the **D**ependent variable is usually the one you **D**on't know. The Inde-pendent variable is the one that you (**I**) have decided when to measure.
- Know the difference between these **three sorts of variable**:
- **Categoric** – things are sorted into categories, like colour of eyes, or male and female. There's no particular order.
- **Ordered** variables are things like shoe size or age. There is an obvious sequence to this sort of variable.
- **Continuous** variables are things that have a large possible range of values, and a clear sequence. Examples of continuous variables are height in cm, weight in g, amount of gas given off etc.
- Always ask yourself if an experiment is 'valid'. Does the experiment answer the question asked at the start?

Scientific enquiry skill cards

Card 4 – Is this you?

- I know what the line of best fit is and I use it correctly.
- I can identify anomalous results in my own and other graphs.
- I can say what the independent and dependent variables are in investigations.
- When I plan experiments, I choose equipment carefully to increase accuracy, for example choosing a graduated pipette rather than a measuring cylinder for small quantities of liquids.
- I can evaluate my experimental planning and identify and explain possible causes of error.
- I understand that sometimes I don't have enough data or evidence to draw a conclusion. In these situations I can say this and suggest what further information needs to be collected.
- I do calculations on my data to find out things like the rate of reaction, or the average.

These things will help you improve

- Understand and use these two terms:

■ **Interpolate:** using a graph, find out information from a data point that lies between two of the points on your graph.

■ **Extrapolate**: extend the line of best fit beyond the last point to find a data point that lies beyond the range of data you collected during the experiment.

- **Always look at graphs critically** – do the points lie close to the line of best fit? If they don't you might wonder if the experiment was carried out accurately. When repeats have been carried out, are the results close to each other for every trial of the experiment? If not, you might wonder how reliable the results are.

- Try explaining to a friend how to extrapolate or interpolate data points from a graph.

- When planning, consider what possible equipment there is to measure with, then try to choose the equipment that allows you to measure with the highest degree of accuracy.

Scientific enquiry skill cards

Card 5 – Is this you?

- **I can interpolate and extrapolate data points from graphs.**
- **I can suggest reasons for anomalous points on graphs.**
- **I can identify the variables in an experiment, identify the dependent and independent variable, and suggest which variables should be changed and which should stay the same in order to collect valid data.**
- **I plan to make my experiments reliable by repeating readings.**
- **I can look critically at someone else's experimental method and data and suggest improvements to the method to increase reliability and accuracy.**

These things will help you improve

- Always look for ways to comment on how you could **improve the accuracy** (how close to the true value your results are) **or reliability** (how sure you are that you would get the same result if you did the experiment over again) of an experiment. Make sure you know the difference between accuracy and reliability.
- **Be critical** of your own and others' experimental procedures; evaluation is often poorly dealt with and yet it is the path to improvement!
- **Look for clues** in graphs and tables that help you to see where mistakes have been made. Try to work out what in the experimental method could have happened to cause each anomaly.

Source: The progression in group talk activity was developed from an original idea by the National Strategies: Progressing to level 6 and beyond.

The problem

I want to make use of engaging contemporary contexts in my work

A solution

Using ICT

The study of science offers enormous potential for the use of engaging and exciting contemporary contexts. Please do not fall into the trap of feeling that the way to use contemporary contexts is to bring in a pile of newspapers and ask pupils to highlight important points. There might be a place for that, but in terms of engagement and excitement, it doesn't feature in my top ten.

Here are some of the ways you can get pupils to engage with contemporary contexts – there are more in the section on Developing writing.

Using You Tube

You Tube is full of brilliant and exciting examples of how people use science in their work and in their lives. These clips can be used is a variety of ways. You can use You Tube as a basis for group discussion, for example

1 What science is being used here?

2 How important is science in helping this person do their job?

3 What are the risks here and how are they being managed?

4 Did this job exist 5 or 10 years ago?

If you type 'high voltage cable testing' into the You Tube search engine, a series of videos will appear that describe the job of a cable tester who spends his days crawling among the mains cables that are strung between pylons. You can find an amazing video with a good commentary. It provides a great 'jumping off' point (if you'll pardon the pun) for a discussion about managing risk and the application of science theories to real-life situations.

Using Photo Story 3

Photo Story 3 is a free download; you will find it if you type the name into an internet search engine. It is a brilliant little programme that allows you to use photographs, text, music and voiceovers to create a short video. Beware – Photo Story can be addictive!

A good way to use Photo Story is to encourage group talk that helps pupils to make progress along the strand of the Framework that develops their understanding of developing explanations. The objective here is to help pupils understand that different explanations can arise from individual bias.

Choose the topic area that you are addressing; for example from the 'Changing Environment and sustainability' topic, you might choose to explore the potential impacts of genetically modified (GM) crops on the environment, and on the supply of world food. See case study overleaf.

Ways to use Photo Story 3

● To summarise key ideas about a topic
● To explain how scientists worked together to come to a conclusion
● To start a discussion about 'questions science cannot answer'
● To produce a TV-style report about a current news item
● With digital photos of the pupils carrying out a practical as a report on their findings
● After a special event to celebrate achievement

I'm sure you can think of many more.

Photo Story 3 case study

1 Prepare a folder of no more than 20 relevant photographs (make sure the file names of the photos are helpful. For example, 'Field of GM crops in Ghana' is more useful to the pupils than 'Crops 2') and place them in a folder on your computer desktop.

2 Prepare an information sheet with statements about the issue under discussion. The statements should be bland, but true. For example, 'Some people are concerned that GM crops may damage the environment' and 'Some GM crops are more tolerant to drought'. Make sure there is a balance of statements in favour and against the issue.

3 Choose two pieces of music, one upbeat and one downbeat.

4 Group pupils into threes and give them a 'storyboard'. A storyboard has 12 empty rectangles on it and a group is only allowed one storyboard between them. Immediately you are starting to ask them to be selective about the information and pictures they are using.

5 Give out the information sheets to each group.

6 Either assign viewpoints to groups or allow them to choose whether they are 'pro' or 'anti' GM crops.

7 Ask pupils to design a TV advert to support their point of view, using only the pictures and information that they have been given. Pupils should write the words or pictures that they are using for each frame into the storyboard.

8 Using a storyboard in this way eliminates the problem of the pupils focusing on the technology rather than the learning. The learning takes pace as the pupils negotiate and make decisions about which pictures and text will best persuade others to take their point of view.

9 An effective next step is to ask the groups to make up their Photo Story at home in preparation for the next lesson. This requires a good school ICT infrastructure so that the pupils can access the resources from home or from the school library. Alternatively, one or two groups could make their Photo Story and share it with the class, or you could arrange to use an ICT room for 15 minutes – it really doesn't take any longer than that.

10 The crucial last step for this activity is to reflect on the learning. What made the different videos effective? How did they choose the information and pictures to use? What thinking did they go through? How does this relate to the way that people think about other scientific issues?

The outcome of this discussion could be used to devise criteria with which to judge other Photo Story activities in the future.

Pupils using Photo Story 3 share their video with the class.

TITLE :

GM
GOOD OR
BAD?

TEXT

SOME GM CROPS
CAN GROW IN
VERY DRY
CLIMATES

PICTURE

FIELD OF
CROPS

TEXT

THAT MEANS
THAT IN TIMES
OF DROUGHT....

TEXT

...PEOPLE DON'T
HAVE TO GO
HUNGRY

PICTURE

FEEDING
STATION, NAMIBIA

PICTURE

FARMER
HARVESTING
CROPS

TEXT

SOME GM CROPS
ARE MORE
RESISTANT TO
PESTS

PICTURE

LOCUST

TEXT

MEANING FARMERS
CAN USE LESS
CHEMICALS

TEXT

GM - GOOD OR
BAD?
WHAT DO YOU
THINK?

PICTURE

?

Using a storyboard to record their decisions about what will be in the video keeps the learners focused.

Section 3: **Developing group talk**

The problem

My small group won't talk

My small group won't talk on task

I don't know what to talk about!

A solution

Conversation cube

Pupils love to have something to manipulate and hold while they are thinking or talking. A foam cube with a plastic cover is a brilliant tool to help to facilitate talk. A supplier of such cubes (they call them 'Giant Pocket Dice) is www.craftpacks.co.uk. The cube has been used extremely successfully with all types of learners. It will help you to support a small group instead of an individual, and increase the confidence of the learners in their group talk.

Ideas on how to use the cube to encourage learning conversations

1 **Have six pictures or diagrams on the faces of the cube. Pupils have to describe the science behind whatever picture they throw.**

2 **There are six pieces of evidence to support an argument or hypothesis. Each pupil has a cube with all pieces of evidence on. Pupils choose the piece of evidence that they feel is the strongest supporting evidence and then have to justify their decision to their peers.**

3 **Use the cube as a speaking object, i.e. whoever is holding the cube can speak, and the rest of the group listen.**

4 **Have De Bono's thinking hats on the cube, one hat on each side (see page 76).**

The Yellow Hat is sunny and positive. Be hopeful and optimistic.

5 **Put an expression on each side and use it to describe an emotion. Pupils can use the cube to communicate how they themselves are feeling, or an emotional response to an issue that is being discussed.**

6 **Use the cube to model expectations and what should be happening. For example, have a picture for each classroom activity and use the**

visual cue to redirect the pupil to the required activity. Suggestions for each face are: reading; listening; thinking; pair talk; group discussion; writing.

7 **In group work, have each pupil's name and photo on one side of the cube. Use a cube throw to determine who answers each question. This encourages pupils to remain engaged. An alternative is to use the pupil who is 'selected' by the cube to ask a suitable question of another pupil.**

8 **Put a picture and name of a common piece of apparatus on each side of the cube and ask what they can be used for (you could use the Equipment cards from earlier in this chapter for this).**

9 **Put the name and a diagram of a process on each face of the cube and ask what the process is used for. Pupils can also describe the pieces of apparatus used for each process.**

10 **Odd one out: On five faces, put names or pictures of things that are similar, and on one face, something that is different. Pupils identify the odd one out and justify their decisions.**

11 **Place a different graph shape on each of the faces and ask pupils to discuss what the axes might be.**

12 **Place different graphs on each face and ask pupils to tell the story of the line.**

13 **Use a picture or cartoon as a stimulus. Have the words Which, Why, How, Where, When and Who on the six faces of the cube. Pupils throw the cube and then have to ask a question with the appropriate starting word. (see page 77).**

14 **Have a Key Idea (Cells, Forces, Interdependence, Energy, Particles) on each face; pupils have to use that key idea to explain an observation. On the last face, put 'You choose'. They can then use any of the key ideas to explain the observation.**

15 **On opposite faces of the cube are the name of a state and a particle diagram. One or more could be missing, ask pupils to draw or write the missing part on a sticky note and place it in the appropriate place.**

16 **The cube could be used for a revision activity, with a question on each side. Pupil would take it in turns to roll the cube and answer the questions that came up.**

17 **A key word for the topic could be written on each side and the pupils have to explain what the key word means.**

18 **Fill in some of the faces and leave others blank. Pupils have to discuss what might be on the missing faces. This could be useful in helping pupils to identify and explain patterns.**

De Bono's Six Thinking Hats

The Red Hat

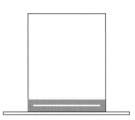

represents anger (seeing red).
Listen to your emotions, your intuition.

The Blue Hat

is the colour of the sky, high above us all.
Look from a higher and wider perspective.

The Black Hat

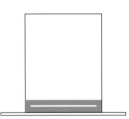

is gloomy and negative.
Look at why this will fail.

The Yellow Hat

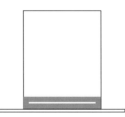

is sunny and positive.
Be hopeful and optimistic.

The Green Hat

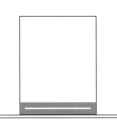

is grass, fertile and growing.
Be creative and cultivate new ideas.

The White Hat

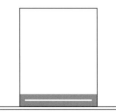

is cold, neutral, and objective.
Look at the facts and figures.

Prompts to use on a conversation cube

? Who	**?** What
? Where	**?** Why
? How	**?** When

The problem

When my group talk, they argue!

A solution

Conversation cards

Supporting pupils to work as groups

Talk helps students to learn. It is an extremely important tool, but often the pupils who most need to develop these skills don't know how they can do this. Make it easy for them by scaffolding the activity.

Being able to talk about the applications and implications of science is important; it is crucial that pupils are confident in expressing their point of view about how science might affect society. A good understanding of the area 'implications of science' is part of the KS3 Programme of study and the KS4 Programme of study.

For example, in the Framework for Teaching Science, pupils are asked to 'Explain how bias, a lack of evidence or misconceptions can give rise to different explanations', and to 'Identify the limitations in a range of scientific explanations'. One of the yearly learning objectives in the Framework for year 7 pupils is that they should 'Recognise that decisions about the use and application of science and technology are made by society and individuals and can impact on the way people think and behave'. These are important areas for pupils to understand and are effectively explored using group talk. However, pupils often lack the skill to explore ideas in this way and the tools below to go some way towards addressing this.

Often conversations between pupils will remain at the most basic level – pupils will imitate the conversational type that they see around them, and some pupils need to be taught in school to have in-depth, exploratory conversations. We can help them to develop this by modelling how it might look with other pupils and adults.

The most basic stage of conversation can be labelled the 'I think this and if you disagree you're wrong' stage. Here, pupils take up opposing positions and will not budge from their positions. This type of conversation can lead to anger and even aggression as the views become more entrenched. Pupils in this stage lack the negotiating skills to move on.

You might hear

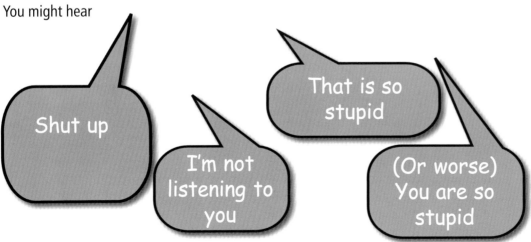

Basic conversation

Here is an example of this sort of conversation, on this occasion in a class discussing whether nuclear power stations might be a good way to meet our energy needs:

Sean 'I think they are a good idea … yeah, we should build more of them.'

Faye 'No! They're bad! They shouldn't build more – they should build more windmills and things… things that are better.'

Jamie 'You can't get enough energy from them. Nuclear power stations make more power so they should build them.'

Faye 'You are such an idiot. You don't care what happens to the world, do you?'

Jamie 'I'm just saying the facts.'

Sean 'Yeah, at least he's not a hippie. Why don't you go and dance round a tree or something.'

The next stage could be referred to as the 'I don't agree but at least I'm not being rude' stage. Pupils are starting to listen to each other, and at least acknowledge that others can hold opposing views. The feeling can often be that the majority view must be the 'right' one – it can provoke interesting discussions if you raise this question – because a lot of people think the same thing, does that make it right?

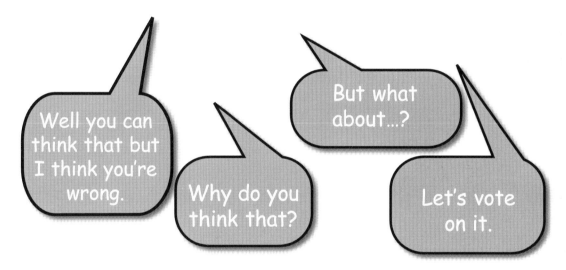

Pupils start to listen to the other speakers

Here is another classroom conversation, this time about genetic engineering.

Erin 'So, what do you all think? I think it is ok to genetically engineer stuff as long as it's not for food.'

Jay 'But isn't that half the point – to make plants that will grow food in places where other stuff won't grow?'

Erin 'Yeah but I wouldn't want to eat it.'

Jay 'Why – nobody has found that it is bad for you.'

Mia 'Just because nobody has found it out yet doesn't mean it's not bad for you. What about that drug they gave to people that made them have deformed babies!'

Jay 'This is only food – it's not like a drug that can kill you.'

Mia 'I'm just saying they don't know that yet.'

Rashid 'Well I still wouldn't eat it.'

At the next stage, things really become exciting. As pupils enter this stage, they really are making great progress in their conversation and reasoning skills. They are beginning to appreciate that the views of other people might be valuable and that they might learn from them. Pupils may say things like:

And here is a discussion on stem cell research.

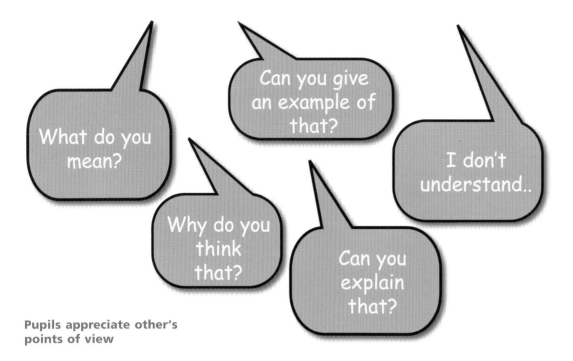

Pupils appreciate other's points of view

Dave 'I don't know whether it's ok or not – I think it depends what you use it for.'

Mark 'Do you think it is ok to use embryos though – I mean, they're like babies, aren't they?'

Kim 'They can't use them after 14 days – that's when the nerves start developing so.... so.. are they alive? When is something alive?'

Mark 'I think they are alive straight... as soon as the egg is fertilised.'

Kim 'But the embryos that are used are spare ones – so they wouldn't get to live anyway.'

Dave 'Where do they get them from?'

Kim 'I think they use ones that are left over from fertility treatment. They get chucked out otherwise.'

Mark 'I agree with Dave and I suppose it depends what they are used for... like do they help people with disease or just help people, like, look better or something? I think it's ok if they are helping to cure people.'

Although sometimes it can feel like an uphill battle, there are ways that you can help pupils to develop their talk into something useful and meaningful that will move them on in their learning. Here are some ways to help pupils to make progress in their group talk skills.

A solution

Group talk progression cards

It will really help if you can show students what good group work looks like and the sorts of things that they might say to each other in successful group work. For example, the progression below illustrates the sort of things that pupils might say at different stages of effectiveness in group work.

The idea of the cards is that the pupils have the card that corresponds to the level above where they are. I would not recommend giving out the stage 1 card; just use it to show what pupils do when they need to work on their group talk. If pupils are at this basic level, it's worth using a different strategy, such as conversation cards, to develop their skills and then start using the progression cards at stage 2.

Source: The progression in group talk activity was developed from an original idea by the National Strategies: Progressing to level 6 and beyond.

I'm improving at group talk

I say things like:

'I think…because'
'Have you thought of…'
'I disagree, because…'
'But what about…'
'How does… fit into…'

- I can work as part of a small or large group.
- I contribute to the group discussion.
- I listen to what others say.
- I can make comments that respond to what others have said.
- I am learning how to disagree with others without upsetting them.
- I understand and can explain how working in a group helps to develop my thinking.
- I can ask questions that help others to explain their thinking.

I'm taking group talk further

I say things like:

'I do see your point, but have you thought about…'
'I think we need to move on from this point. Shall we think about…'
'So I think what you are saying is… Am I right?'
'Suzy, what do you think about…?'
'I hadn't thought of that. I think that means…'

- I can work as part of groups with people I don't know well.
- I can disagree with others without upsetting them.
- I can summarise what others have said.
- I can ask questions that help move the discussion on.
- I can clearly explain my point of view in a variety of ways.
- I can suggest ways to move the discussion on when it gets 'stuck'.
- My view sometimes changes because of what someone else has said.
- I can see how the group works, and help to include people who are reluctant to join in.

I'm confident and skilled at group talk

I say things like:

'Would anyone like to start off by summarising what the
question is that we're discussing?'
'We need to keep an eye on the time…'
'What are the main issues here?'
'When you said.., did you mean…'
'Have I understood you correctly when you said…'
'Sorry, I'm confused. Could you go over that point again?'
'I think that is the same as… Am I right?'
'I think that is different to… because… Am I right?'
'Anything to add, Ali?'
'Do you agree with Rashid, Jack, or is there something else you'd like to say?'
'How can we move on from here?'
'We need to make sure everyone has their say. Shall we try using a talking object?'
'I think if we jotted a few things down, it would help to clarify our thoughts. Shall we try that?'

- I understand the different roles that I can take in a group (like chairperson, spokesperson, timekeeper), and I can carry out any of these roles.
- I know and can organise lots of different ways of working in groups.
- I can see which method of group working is appropriate for different situations.
- I can ask questions that help everyone in the group understand.
- I can help the group to come to joint conclusions.
- I can see how other people's thinking fits into my own and where it is different, and then explore this.
- I can see where the group is working well and where improvement is needed.
- I can take action to address the weaknesses of a group.

A solution

Group work bingo

These prompt cards help pupils to have ideas about what to say in group talk conversations. They are a simple version of the 'Conversation Cards' (see page 87). Give each pupil a set of the cards printed on a 'bingo' card. When each pupil has used each phrase appropriately, the group can call 'bingo'. This may cause some silliness at first, but it will certainly help pupil rehearse the sorts of phrases that support effective group talk.

Group work bingo

Group work bingo cards

I think…	Can you explain that again…	I'd like to hear what… thinks.
What do you think…	Have you thought of…	Can someone sum up what's been said?
I agree with…	I think the main point is…	I need more information about…
I disagree, because…	I'm confused about…	Can you give an example of…

A solution

Word tennis (or volleyball, if you have a big group!)

This game will help pupils to start to read each other's visual clues and also start to build their confidence as a group.

The aim is to complete a 'rally' of as many words as you can before you get 'stuck'. Start off by saying a word. Someone else in the group has to say a word that is associated with it. Students will have to watch each other to make sure two people don't talk at the same time. The game continues until you ring a bell, at which point the last person to speak has to justify the association that they made between the last two words. If they can do it, they get 2 points, and the game continues where it left off. If two pupils talk at the same time, they can lose points, and when they have lost a certain number, they are out.

As the students get better at it you can use more advanced scientific vocabulary. Students are encouraged to make links between different areas of the topic – a higher level skill.

Example:	
Teaching assistant:	**Beaker**
Jo:	**Water**
Heidi:	**Oxygen**
Ryan:	**Breathing**
Sam:	**Bones**
Teaching assistant:	**(rings bell) Sam, can you make a link between those last two, breathing and bones, please?**
Sam:	**When you breathe in, your rib cage has to lift to make the air go in – you couldn't breathe without bones.**
Teaching assistant:	**What do you all think? 2 points? (the group votes yes) OK – Sam do you want to start us off again?**
Sam:	**Liver**
Donna:	**Stomach**

And so the game goes on. As well as emphasising the links between topics and rehearsing the use of key words, the game helps to develop the pupils' use of verbal cues. Pupils don't take it in turn around the circle, they have to watch each other to make sure they don't talk at the same time.

Games like word volleyball help pupils to learn to listen to each other.

A solution

Conversation cards

Make yourself a set of 'group work' cards, see page 88. When you work with a small group, put the cards in the middle of the table. Encourage students to take a card from the middle of the table. The card has a sentence start on it – the students can have some time to think and then come up with their sentences and take it in turns to talk.

The students get points as a group for keeping the conversation going, and points mean prizes.

Start practicing the technique with a topic that the students are comfortable with. Some suitable starters for conversations might be…

- **What is your favourite TV programme and why?**
- **Which is a better pet, a cat or a dog, and why?**
- **How do you make a cup of tea?**
- **Which is better, peanut butter or jam? Why?**
- **What would you do if you won the lottery?**
- **If you could only eat one food for the rest of your life, what would you choose and why?**

The conversations will be extremely stilted and difficult to start with – students may giggle or be reluctant to speak at first. Keep the tone light and relaxed – remember the students are probably right at the edge of their comfort zone. Practice makes perfect!

Once students have had a few goes and the conversation is running a bit more freely, let the students decide on a topic to talk about. When the students have practiced this for a while (but before they become bored – you will know when the right time to move on is), change the activity. The students might have noticed and commented on the different colours of the cards. Can they work out what they mean? What effect do the different colours on the cards have on the conversation? Can they explain why?

The cards are coloured by the effect that they have on the conversation. The red cards are conversation-stoppers – they keep the conversation at the most basic level and nobody can move on or develop their ideas. The yellow cards help to develop ideas and help to move the conversation on. The green cards are the most advanced, and are a bit more difficult to use, bacause they often require students to summarise what others have said.

Use every opportunity to use the conversation cards for a couple of weeks. Try talking about these science topics using the conversation cards.

- **Which is the best important invention and why, TV or mobile phones?**
- **Why should we recycle?**
- **Which is more important and why, exercise or a healthy diet?**
- **Should the public decide what scientists investigate?**
- **Are there some experiments that scientists shouldn't do? Why?**
- **What is the most important thing that science has discovered? Why?**

Conversation cards

 R

'I think *(say what you think)* and I don't care what you think.'

 R

'How can you think that?'

 G

'I do see your point, but have you thought about *(suggest something else)*'

 Y

'What are the main issues here?'

G

'I hadn't thought of that. I think that means *(say what you think it means).*'

 G

'I think that is the same as *(say what you think)* Am I right?'

G

'Would anyone like to start off by summarising what the question is that we're discussing?'

G

'Do you agree with *(say the name of who just spoke), (say the name of someone who has been quiet so far),* or is there something else you'd like to say?'

 Y

'How can we move on from here?'

 Y

'I think if we jotted a few things down, it would help to clarify our thoughts. Shall we try that?'

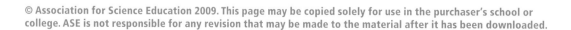

G

'I think that is different to *(say what you think it is different to)* because *(say why)*. Am I right?'

 Y

'When you said *(say what they said)*, did you mean *(say what you thought they meant)*.'

 Y

'We need to keep an eye on the time…'

 G

'*(Say the name of someone who hasn't said much yet)*, what do you think about *(what you're talking about)?*'

 G

'So I think what you are saying is *(say what you think they are saying)*.

Am I right?'

 Y

'But what about…'

 Y

'I think *(say what you think)* because *(say why you think it)*.'

R

'You're wrong *(say why you think they are wrong)*.'

G

'We need to make sure everyone has their say. Shall we try using a talking object?'

 Y

'Anything to add *(say the name of someone who hasn't said much yet)?*'

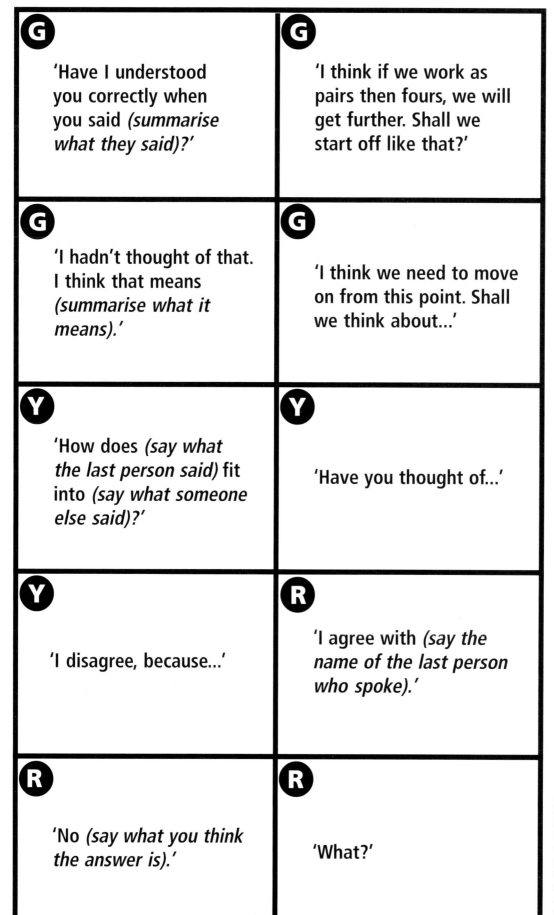

G 'Have I understood you correctly when you said *(summarise what they said)?'*

G 'I think if we work as pairs then fours, we will get further. Shall we start off like that?'

G 'I hadn't thought of that. I think that means *(summarise what it means).'*

G 'I think we need to move on from this point. Shall we think about...'

Y 'How does *(say what the last person said)* fit into *(say what someone else said)?'*

Y 'Have you thought of...'

Y 'I disagree, because...'

R 'I agree with *(say the name of the last person who spoke).'*

R 'No *(say what you think the answer is).'*

R 'What?'

e-resource

Section 4: **Developing writing**

The problem

The student I'm working with won't write

A solution

Record achievement in other ways

Many pupils find writing difficult and frustrating, and it can be a source of great friction between pupils and teachers. The reason for reluctance on the part of some learners to engage with writing can be better understood with an analogy.

Imagine you were really great at many things to do with driving your car. You drove extremely safely, had never been in an accident and had built up seven years of no claims bonus with your insurance company. You knew and applied all the rules of the road. Imagine you knew everything there was to know about car maintenance and you could fix your car no matter what problem arose. Imagine you spent a lot of your free time on the internet researching makes and models of cars and you could give good advice to other people about which cars were most economical and where to go for the best service at a garage. Your knowledge, understanding and application of cars and driving is almost complete…. but…. you can't parallel park.

So in your everyday life, you avoid occasions when you know you'll have to parallel park. You choose places to go to shop that have car parks; you make sure that you have a house with off-road parking. You buy a car that has power steering to help you with your parking. And when you can't avoid it, you parallel park. It takes you longer than it would to park in a car park, and you find it stressful and have to be extra careful, but you manage it.

But then imagine that you have to take an advanced drivers test to get a job that you want as a salesperson for a car company. You know that you would sail through all the sections – except the parking. You look at the information about the test and…. every single section is to be assessed by your ability to parallel park quickly and confidently. You have to explain how an engine works to the examiner – while parallel parking. You have to describe how economical different cars are – while parallel parking. The final part of the test examines your motorway driving – but you can only pass that section if, at the end of it, you can parallel park first time in the spot outside the driving school office on your return.

Now, there are two possible routes to take here. The first is, of course, to improve your parallel parking. To practice and practice and practice until you know you can get it right first time every time. Those who are confident and have had success with learning before may well choose to go down this route.

The second route is to give up. You'd decide that the testing was unreasonable and unfair and that you wanted no part of it. You might choose this response if you had lower self-confidence and hadn't had much success previously.

Now put yourself in the shoes of our reluctant writers. Most likely they haven't had a huge amount of success in school so far. Most likely they have previously felt judged on what they haven't been able to do rather than what they have been able to do (or it may have felt like that to them). Some reluctant writers are extremely able verbally, and very competent at using a computer to communicate. They may be extremely articulate. They may be able to visualise and describe and conjure up complex abstract models in their head. They may be able to make presentations to their peers that are both amusing and informative. They may be able to type at 30 words per minute when messaging their friends online. They may be able to do all these things, but they find writing difficult and frustrating. And now they are being asked, in many of their lessons, to be judged almost entirely on the one thing that they find most difficult. Is it any surprise they are frustrated?

Now don't misunderstand me; I am not saying that pupils shouldn't be asked to write or that writing isn't important – in fact it is extremely important that pupils are able to write extended explanations in science. Many pupils struggle with this and an inability to write extended explanations can be a blocker to pupils reaching levels 6 and 7.

However, I am saying that we live in an increasingly electronic age. Look at me – I've written a whole book and I haven't put pen to paper! Many pupils will find it a lot easier to carry out written tasks using a word processing programme. Where there are opportunities for this, take them. This isn't always possible, but it may help some of the pupils you work with if you encourage the use of ICT.

There are also many ways other than writing to find out where pupils are in their learning. Listening to them explain the science is a good place to start! Once you have a good understanding of Levelness and Gradeness (see chapter 2), you will be able to get an excellent idea of where they are by what they say and the questions they ask.

Here are a variety of other assessment methods where the evidence of the outcome for pupils could be recorded and stored electronically.

Teaching episodes and talks

Some pupils love being in front of their peers and enjoy teaching something to the rest of the class. It is important, if you decide to use this strategy, that you and the pupils agree clear criteria for how the presentation will be judged, otherwise it can be rather unfocused. Teaching episodes and talks are also a great opportunity for pupils to give each other feedback on their work.

Photo Story 3

Photo Story 3 is a brilliant programme by Microsoft that allows pupils to make their own videos with music and voiceovers. It is a free download and it is easy to use. Again, make sure there are clear criteria in place for assessing the video before you ask pupils to produce a report in this way.

Podcasts

Another free download is the 'Audacity' software. This allows you to create audio files that can be saved and used as podcasts. You can add sound effects and jingles to create a 'radio interview' feel if you like. Again, keep it focused on how the learning is being advanced by the activity. If pupils are doing this activity to develop their understanding of how scientists work together to validate theories, make sure that pupils know this and focus on it in their podcast.

Blogs that summarise the learning

Some teachers have had great success with asking pupils to summarise the learning from a lesson in a class 'blog', which can then subsequently be used as revision. You may like to try something like this if you have pupils who would find this engaging.

Annotated digital photographs of the pupil explaining something or showing how something works

This works well and most schools now have a digital camera available. Many pupils have mobile phones that can take photographs that they can download and incorporate in a document or presentation. The pupil does the annotation that explains what they are doing in the pictures and why. Be as inventive as you like with this one – pupils will be keen to engage in writing captions for the pictures you or they have taken.

A commentary or voice over on a video about the topic

Use a section of a science video or a science clip. If your school subscribes to ClipBank or a similar service, you can download a news clip, use Movie Maker from Microsoft to edit it and add a voiceover. Ask pupils to make a commentary for the clip, or suggest what subtitles might be used. Pupils can produce a professional looking video.

A cartoon or storyboard that shows the stages in a process

This one is fairly self-explanatory. A note of caution, though – pupils may spend a long time producing the artwork rather than concentrating on the science learning. If this is likely for the pupil you are working with, do not use the cartoon strip approach. Use the storyboard with a limited number of frames (say, five) and ask pupils first to decide what each of the five frames will be for. Then ask them to write a caption for each frame. To complete the task, pupils illustrate the story as clearly and simply as they can. An example of where this approach can be very effective is when asking pupils to describe what happens to the water molecules during changes of state.

The use of a graphic organiser to categorise and order their understanding

Graphic organisers can be really helpful for pupils who are struggling to marshall their thoughts and see how ideas link together. Making links between areas of science and understanding how ideas about how scientists work feed into our knowledge of science is an important part of reaching the higher levels and grades. There are lots of books on mind maps, concept maps and other ways of organising thinking. Flowcharts are also helpful tools because they encourage pupils to sequence and order ideas.

As you allow pupils to demonstrate their skill and understanding in a variety of ways, their confidence will grow. Provide a wide variety of alternative ways for pupils to be successful and allow writing to come naturally as a result of the increasing confidence that the pupil has in his or her abilities. When pupils feel more confident in themselves as learners and scientists, there are a variety of strategies that you can put in place to support individual pupils in making progress in their writing.

The problem

The student I'm working with can hardly write!

A solution

Sheep and eees!

It is a fact that many of the pupils we work with in schools have never learned a love of writing and find it tiring and difficult. In order to write clearly and fluently, without painful cramp in the hand, learners need to spend time practicing. Writing is something you can encourage the pupil you are supporting to do, both during lessons and at home.

Writing lines of eee's both upside down and the right way up, will help the pupil's hand–eye coordination and increase stamina. Using sheets of normal lined paper is fine, although if the pupil is diligent and wants to keep a track of how fluency and neatness are improving, they could use a notebook so they can look back to see how their writing has changed over time. You can set challenges for the pupil, asking them to complete a set number of pages over the weekend, for example.

To take it further, the pupil can use the looped eee's to draw flowers and sheep; even create a whole landscape. This is the sort of thing that can be done as doodling on the bus or in front of the television, and shouldn't be presented as a chore, more a tool to improve the hand muscles. **Use eees to make patterns and pictures**

Pupils can practice their writing and improve fluency by doodling shapes with eees.

The problem

I don't know what the next steps in writing are for my student

A solution

The writing stepladder

Ways to use the writing stepladder.

- For students to use as a target sheet
- As a way to help maintain consistency of focus for the pupil if you work in a team of TAs
- As a prompt for you to focus on the areas that will move the pupils on in writing
- For more able pupils to develop their skills if you work with them individually or as a small group
- As a focus for a small group for a period of time.
- As a source of ideas when you're out of inspiration
- As a working electronic document as part of the electronically-help records on the pupil
- As a way of passing information on the pupil's progress to others who support the pupil
- As a reminder of areas of focus for parents and carers to work on with their child – a link between the school and home.

Developing a pupil's skill in writing can help him improve across all subjects.

I'm on the starting blocks

Is this you?

- Written questions sometimes confuse me.
- I sometimes know the answers, but I find it hard to put my ideas into writing.
- I don't know the difference between 'describe' and 'explain'.
- I often don't finish work I'm set, or tests.

Then try this to improve...

- Read the question to yourself out loud.
- Talk through your answers (in your head if you need to). Keep doing it until your answer makes sense.
- Get someone to talk through this difference with you.
- There's only one way to get better at something – practice! Write whenever you can; including doodling in front of the TV. A chain of the letter e, sheep and flowers are really good ways to practice your pen control.

WRITING

Make sure pupils are given opportunities to demonstrate what they can do in a variety of ways – not just though writing.

I'm improving my writing in science

Is this you?

- I know the science key language for the topic I am working on.
- I use the science key words when I am making explanations verbally.
- I use the science key words when I am writing.
- My written work includes some relevant detail, for example, I might be able to explain how the key ideas fit together.

Then try this to improve...

- Make sure you can describe in detail what the key words for each topic mean.
- When you explain things verbally, or in writing, always include the appropriate scientific language.
- You should include examples and make links between the key science ideas in your explanations.

I'm starting out at writing in science

Is this you?

- I'm not sure what the key science language is for the topic I'm studying.
- I sometimes use key science words when I am talking in science.
- I sometimes use key science words when I am writing in science.
- I can write short answers but I'm not really sure I'm using the science key words correctly. where you have put them.

Then try this to improve...

- Ask what the key words are for the topic and make sure you know what they mean.
- Aim to include some of the key words in each verbal explanation you make.
- When writing, think about which are the most important things you have to say, and work out the key science words you need. Then include them.
- Read through your work to make sure the key words make sense

The writing stepladder

I'm confident and skilled in scientific writing

Is this you?

- I can select the appropriate information from different sources (for example; scientific publications, reliable internet sources).
- I can use this information to explain or develop a point about science.
- I can write appropriately with a particular audience in mind (for example, an information sheet about foods to avoid during pregnancy; a scientific report to a company on a product in development), explaining scientific terminology where appropriate.
- I include evidence in my written work and comment on the reliability of the evidence.
- I understand how to use evidence and references to synthesise and support an argument.

Then try this to improve...

- You need to be able to explain why some websites are more reliable than others. Can you?
- Make sure you write a rough plan before you start your longer explanation. This will help you to organize your thinking.
- Think carefully about your audience – what science do they need to know and why? You need to be able to explain and justify why you included and excluded particular information or vocabulary.
- You could improve your skills in scientific writing by looking at some published scientific papers.
- Try using an internet search engine to find information about 'writing scientific research papers'.

I'm taking scientific writing further

Is this you?

- I always use appropriate scientific language in my explanations and when I evaluate evidence or experiments.
- I know how to structure explanations so they make sense to the person reading my work.
- My verbal explanations are logical and make sense to the listener.
- I can produce longer pieces of written work on my own.
- I know the difference between opinion and fact and can make this clear in my writing.
- I can use written work to express logically both sides of an argument and then explain what I think and why.

Then try this to improve...

- When you evaluate experiments, make sure you refer to how reliable the data was, and why.
- It helps to talk through the structure of your written work before you start (even if you have to talk to yourself!).
- Write a rough plan of your work first, it helps to structure your thinking.
- When writing or talking about evidence and opinion, some useful words and phrases are: however, nevertheless, on the contrary, in support of this, contradicting this, on the other side of the argument, despite this, my opinion is, I agree with this because, I disagree with this because.

The problem

The student I'm working with doesn't know the scientific language to use

A solution

The hotel bell

Hotel bell

A key part of a pupil reaching level 3 and beyond in science, as well as in other subjects is to be able to use the correct terminology accurately and appropriately.

A good way to encourage pupils to do this is to put in place two things. Firstly, you need to produce a list of the important scientific vocabulary that the pupil should be using during the lesson. Secondly, you need to introduce some sort of recognition when the pupil uses the words appropriately.

The list of key words should be short – perhaps between five and ten words for a series of two or three lessons. Make sure the pupil knows what the words mean to start with. This would be a good activity to carry out at the start of a topic to check what the pupil already knows, as a review activity or as an alternative to a lesson activity that is unsuitable for the child you are supporting.

Once the pupil is secure in what the words mean, they get a 'ding' (or stickers, or points) every time they use a correct word appropriately. This process reinforces the importance of the correct use of the words and the words themselves. And the pupils are encouraged to engage with the learning as they look for opportunities to use the key language appropriately.

You can buy a 'hotel bell' online for about £5. Use a search engine to search for a 'call bell' to find places that sell them.

The problem

I need some help supporting Centre Marked Assessment and investigations

A solution

Investigation cubes

Many exam boards still use investigations as a way of assessing pupils' practical, analytical and evaluative skills. The practical is planned, carried out and written up by the students, usually over a period of a few weeks. Such assessments are usually marked by the students' class teacher and then moderated by the rest of the department and finally, a sample of the work is checked by the exam board.

Assessed investigations are an important opportunity for students to show what they are capable of, but are often a very challenging activity for some of the students you may be supporting because of the extended concentration and writing they require.

It is very important for you to understand the requirement of your school's exam board for centre marked assessment. Ask the class teacher for a copy of the marking criteria. In many schools, pupils have access to this from the start of the work to help them understand what is required. Many pupils will need the mark scheme interpreted for them.

Once the class has carried out the practical work, it is likely that they will do some kind of write-up. If you are supporting during this, it is a good idea to have some questions in mind to 'open up' the conversation. One way to do this that has proved useful is to use the Foam Cube (see also page 74) as a prop to help you start up conversations with the pupils. A supplier of such cubes (they call them 'Giant Pocket Dice) is www.craftpacks.co.uk

Examples of what might go on each face are found on page 101, and also in the section about supporting extended written work and case studies.

The questions on the cube are a good focus for discussion.

Investigation cube

Ideas

Can you explain…?
What do you think…?
Can you think of an example…?
What might you try…?
What might you measure…?
What do you think will happen
when…?

Equipment

What will you need…?
Can you draw a diagram…?
What are the important scientific
words…?
What do you need to do to stay safe?
Have you got everything you need?
Can you talk me through what you'll be
doing?

Planning

What will you change?
What will you keep the same?
How will you record your results?
What units will you be using?
Can you show me how you will…?
How might you draw the results table?
What do you think will happen and why?
How many times will you measure… and
why?

Recording

What are you measuring?
Why do you need to do it more than
once?
What can you see/smell/feel happening?
Are your results what you expected?
When you've repeated your
measurements, were they the same? Do
you know why/why not?

Analysing

How are you going to present your data?
What will go on the *x*-axis / *y*-axis?
How will you measure the scale?
What will be the title?
Can you see any pattern?
Can you use …er…..er to explain (*i.e.,*
as the temperature gets high**er**, the time
to react gets low**er**)
What has happened?
Did you have to repeat any
measurements? Why?

Concluding and evaluating

Can you explain what happened and use
science to explain why?
Did you expect the pattern that you got?
Are you sure that what you found out is a
real pattern; do you feel confident about
your results?
If you were to do the experiment again,
how would you improve the method or the
way you recorded your results?

The problem

I need help supporting research or Case Studies

These days, information is easy to come by. Typing 'stem cell' into an internet search engine returns over twelve and a half million hits. Students are generally very good at finding information on a topic – after all, it is very easy. What is not so easy, and thus the skill it is so important that they learn, is how to sift and sort through this information. Pupils need to know how to be discerning about the information and the sites they use, and how to craft the information they find into a logical and coherent argument.

A solution

Essay Organiser

The essay organiser is a 'thought tool' to help to structure an essay appropriately. When asking pupils to consider conflicting information and then come to their own conclusions, it is a good idea to limit the information that is available at the outset. One way that works well is to present pupils with three or four photocopies of relevant news articles and ask them to highlight the important information or statistics. Then ask them to convert that into the 'Essay Organiser'. When the information is in the Essay Organiser, the pupil can pinpoint particular areas where more information is needed and be very selective about which websites to visit. It is a good idea to limit the time available for website searching to 15 or 20 minutes.

The Essay Organiser is available on the CD – pupils can fill it in using Word. The organiser can just form an 'organiser' for the essay, or, if pupils are very weak, they may not make huge changes to the responses to the prompt for the final version. Make sure, if you are entering the essay for any sort of assessment that any guidance or support that you have given the student is identified when the piece of work is submitted.

Talking through ideas with pupils can really help to clarify their thinking.

Essay Organiser – template

In this box, type what the words in the title mean.

In this box, give scientific details that are important when you are thinking about this topic.

In this box, explain what has recently changed to make this topic important.

In this box, type the evidence that is available to you. Split it into evidence For and Against if this fits in with the title.

In this box, type what extra evidence you would like to find out online or from other sources.

In this box, type what extra evidence you found out online or from other sources. Do you think any of your sources were biased? Why?

In this box, type what you think – what are your conclusions about this topic?

In this box, type what sources of information you used.

Essay Organiser – Example

Which is better, Organic or Intensive Farming?

In this box, write what extra evidence you found out online or from other sources. Do you think any of your sources were biased? Why?

About 30% of UK food is grown organically.

Organic brown bread costs £1.25 for the cheapest loaf at Tesco, and the cheapest non-organic bread is £0.22. Non-organic is a lot cheaper.

The RSPCA are against intensive farming because they say it is stressful and cruel to the animals who can't behave naturally.

I think the RSPCA might be biased because they are always going to come down on the side of the animals.

In this box, write what you think – what are your conclusions about this topic?

I think that whether organic or intensive farming is better depends on what you mean. If you mean which is better for the animals, then organic farming is better, because the animals have more space and are happier. But if you want or need to grow a lot of food then intensive farming might be better.

Personally I prefer organic food because I care about animal welfare and also my family can afford to buy it. I also don't like the thought of taking in the chemicals that have been sprayed on the crops.

In this box, write what sources of information you used.

RSPCA website
Friends of the Earth website
Times newspaper article
Independent newspaper article
'Organic Farming' by Jasper Mudd

In this box, write what the words in the title mean.

Organic farming uses no chemicals on the plants and no hormones or other drugs except for medicines on animals. It relies a lot more on things like manure and crop rotation instead of fertilisers. Intensive farming uses chemicals and packs animals closer together.

In this box, give scientific details that are important when you are thinking about this topic.

Some chemicals can leach into water causing environmental problems like eutrophication.

Some people think intensive animal farming is cruel. Intensively farmed animals are more stressed and less healthy than organically farmed ones.

Intensive farming can produce more food per unit area than organic farming.

Some people prefer to avoid chemicals on their food.

In this box, explain what has recently changed to make this topic important.

In many countries there is a shortage of food.

Organic farming is becoming more widespread in the UK as people are becoming more interested in what they eat.

People in the UK are quite affluent so they can choose organic food even though it is more expensive.

It is easier to find out how food has been produced because supermarkets have to have clear labelling.

In this box, write the evidence that is available to you.
Split it into evidence For and Against if this fits in with the title.

For Intensive	Against Intensive
Get more food per unit area	Food may have chemicals on
More efficient	Chemicals may harm the environment
Food is cheaper	Food may contain less vitamins

For Organic	Against Organic
Animals happier and healthier	Takes longer and more land to grow meat
No chemicals on food	Less food per unit area
Food more nutritious	Food more expensive
No chemicals in environment	

In this box, write what extra evidence you would like to find out online or from other sources.

How much UK food is grown organically?
How much more expensive is organic food, for example bread?
What does the RSPCA say about intensive farming?

A solution

Research bookmarks

These bookmarks help pupils to keep checking that they are going about the research for their essay or case study in the right way. The bookmarks are double-sided and are designed to be printed out, stuck back-to back and then laminated. Choose the one that is appropriate for your pupil.

Using research bookmarks helps learners to build independence and assess the quality of their work.

Research bookmarks

Research - I'm still on the starting blocks

- I need help to plan where to look for information.
- I need to learn some strategies to change information from one sort to another.
- I need to learn to summarise, using a bullet point list or mind map.

Top Tips to improve

- Talk about places that we can get information from. Make a list of these sources to stick in your book and remind you.
- Practice summarizing text, talk and media clips using bullet point lists, mind or concept maps or any other way that works for you.

Source: The research skills bookmarks were developed from an original idea by the National Strategies: Progressing to Level 6 and Beyond Pilot

Research – I'm starting out

- I can pick out a few bits of data or information that could help me to answer a question.
- I am starting to change information from one form to another (for example put text into my own words).
- I am starting to be able to summarise the main ideas from an article or media clip.

Top Tips to improve

- Use a summary table or writing frame to help you to summarise information.
- Practice putting text from textbooks and websites into your own words.
- You can cut and paste information into a document as a handy place to store it, but NEVER cut and paste information directly into an essay, Case Study or research project. It is cheating and could get you disqualified from exams, and also it is VERY easy to spot!

Research - I'm improving my skills

- I can choose a variety of suitable information and data to answer a question.
- I can make links between ideas I have found out and draw conclusions.
- I can change text into my own words.
- I can change text and other information into other forms; for example, I can change a story into a timeline, or turn a method into a flowchart.

Top Tips to improve

- Practice using data and other information to answer questions in class and homework.
- Use a writing frame to evaluate different evidence and make decisions about whether the evidence supports or refutes the argument.
- Try presenting infor mation in different ways. For example, as bulleted points rather than a paragraph; as an article or leaflet aimed at a different audience.
- When you make a decision based on evidence, justify it by saying why you made the decision you did.
- Remember, you are using this skill in classes other than science! What transferable skills to do with research have you learned in other subjects that would also be useful in science?

I'm taking research skills further

- I know how to select relevant data and information from a variety of sources (e.g. books, the internet, media clips, websites and scientific journals).
- I can use relevant evidence to support or negate (not support) an argument.
- I can easily transform evidence into a variety of formats for different audiences and purposes.
- I can write my arguments in a clear and coherent way, so that other people can understand my thinking.

Top Tips to improve

- Try creating criteria to judge whether the evidence is from a range of sources and then assessing your own and your friends' work.
- Have an opinion on the conclusions that others draw from their research and express them.
- Look at examples of where data has been used to develop theories to help you to understand how scientists change their work in the light of new evidence. For example, the development of the understanding of DNA structure.
- Transform information into a different format and evaluate how effective that format is at getting your message across.
- Include a clear format in your writing, with headings and sub-headings to flag up different parts of the text.

I am confident and skilled at research

- I can change what I think if the evidence suggests that my current opinion is not correct.
- I know what reliability is and can judge how reliable a piece of evidence is.
- I know what validity is and can make decisions about whether an experimental plan or a conclusion of someone else's work is valid or not.
- I can decide what the best format for notetaking or information collection is, according to the audience and purpose for which I am writing.

Top Tips to improve

- When looking at evidence, keep thinking about how it applies to your current knowledge. Is the evidence consistent with your current conclusion? If not, adapt your conclusion to fit in with the evidence and justify why you changed your conclusion.
- Always include considerations about reliability and validity in your writing.
- Always consider the audience and purpose for which you are writing, and make sure the style and layout is appropriate.

Section 5: **An Intervention Programme**

The problem

I have to plan an Intervention Programme – where do I start?

A solution

Start where the pupils are!

The most crucial consideration when you are planning an intervention programme is that you know where the pupils are in their learning. Once that is established, you can plan suitable activities that will move them on.

So these are the steps I would suggest.

> **1 Ask for the names, current levels and target levels for the pupils who have been identified as needing intervention.**
>
> **2 Speak to their teachers about what their specific needs are, and if possible get into some classes and speak to the pupils about their learning during lessons.**
>
> **3 There are a wide variety of resources available for the Secondary national strategies that will help pupils to make progress to the different levels. Also, the *Making Good Progress* (DCSF) series will give specific guidance about the support needed by pupils 'stuck' at particular levels. You can find all the resources by going to http://publications.teachernet.gov.uk and entering 'Making good progress at KS3' into the search engine.**
>
> **4 Draw on these resources to provide a tailored intervention programme for the pupils.**
>
> **5 Make sure pupils know what they are learning and why it's important for them.**
>
> **6 Monitor the progress of each pupil, and adjust the programme as needed.**
>
> **7 Make sure the class teacher knows what you and the pupil are focusing on so that this can be built on in their science lessons.**

The ideas and activities I've presented in this chapter are just a starting point. As you become familiar with using the strategies in this chapter, you will want to adapt and add to them for the classes and pupils you are working with.

You will also probably start to generate a variety of strategies yourself – and I would love to hear about them!

Chapter 5 explores ways that you might like to take things further; for your classes, for your school and for yourself.

'Change comes from small initiatives which work, initiatives which imitated, become the fashion.

    We cannot wait for great visions from great people, for they are in short supply at the end of history. It is up to us to light our own small fires in the darkness.'

                                          Charles Handy

Chapter 5   Taking it further

Objective

- To explore how good practice can be spread through the department and school.
- To describe some of the next steps teaching assistants can take in their professional development.

You will probably feel comfortable trying out some of the strategies and ideas suggested in this book straight away. Others will need 'working up to'. This is, of course, completely natural – some of the activities and ideas will be within your current comfort zone, and some outside.

    This chapter asks you to step outside your comfort zone in some other ways too. It suggests ways of developing your practice and some professional development options you might like to consider for the future.

    You may not feel ready to share your good practice now, but, once you are working effectively, have a great understanding of progression and a variety of strategies to move learners on, I'd like you to share them! Share them with your colleagues in the department first of all and then take your show on the road. Don't be afraid to share your new ways of working with other departments in the school – imagine the difference you will make when every teaching assistant in your school is as enthusiastic and skilled as you now are.

    The first time you step up in a meeting to share your new ways of working, you may feel nervous, uncomfortable or out of your depth. This is a great sign; it means you have left your comfort zone. And outside your comfort zone is where you learn and grow.

Taking it further for the classes you support

A good way to try something new is initially with a pupil or a small group that you feel comfortable with. Try the resource or strategy, ask for some feedback from the pupils, change it a bit, and try it again and so on, until you feel happy with the activity. Once you feel confident, then you can try the activity with a different group, or a whole class. Remember, sometimes when you try something new, things seem to get more difficult before they work well. Think back to learning to drive, first on straightforward roads and then encountering your first roundabout; or think of a child moving from crawling to walking. You would not get far if you never mastered roundabouts, or gave up with walking because it just seemed too much of a risk!

Once you begin working closely with a department, there is a common pattern that is likely to prevail, at least initially. Even if you have good support from the Head of Department with clear expectations of the way you should be involved in the department, the chances are this won't happen, at least not straight away. People need time to develop new ways of working and some teachers will need additional encouragement.

Often what will happen is that one or two enthusiastic teachers will work particularly effectively with you – these teachers will provide you with golden opportunities to show what you can do! Other staff may be more reticent and may not use you as effectively. In the worst-case scenario, they may ignore you or just direct you to 'sit with' a particular pupil without giving further guidance. Try not to get too worked up about this – you know how great you are and how much you can help – but you need to convince the teacher that directing you is not an extra 'job', but a huge opportunity. Don't worry – you will win them round!

Back to your enthusiasts – when you are supporting in their classes, you may be able to try things out, discuss activities you have tried or come up with plans to move the learning on for pupils. It is really important that you are a bit of a self-starter with this and happy to take the initiative. Spend time working on some of the strategies that you think will be particularly useful for the pupils at your school, until you are really confident with them.

Once you have got the ball rolling, and you are successfully trying out new activities with the individuals and groups, you will be amazed how even the initially reticent teachers quickly start to come on board. They will see the impact you are having with the pupils you are supporting. Teachers are sometimes reluctant to try new things, partly because they feel under pressure and feel that they cannot take on anything else. Once teachers see that you have got lots of your own ideas, and what is more they are really moving the pupils on in their learning, they will want to be part of it.

Even quite resistant staff can be encouraged to engage with you, if you know how to go about it. Choose a time when they are fairly relaxed and not tearing their hair out over the latest batch of marking or set of reports. If your department has a 'cake day' that can be a good time to chat; most staff can be persuaded to take a 20 minute break by a well-placed Victoria sponge. Ask them if there is anything you can do to help in the next lesson you will be sharing. Try to get them to tell you what they are planning. If they can't think of anything they would like you to do to help, or if they just give you a vague 'If you could sit by John and keep him out of trouble', make a suggestion about something you could do that might lighten their load. You could show them some of your ideas and ask if it is OK to use some of the strategies with the pupils you are working with. Maybe you could start to use the strategies unprompted in appropriate situations with pupils in other classes. The strategies in this book are designed to be used in a wide variety of contexts; it doesn't matter if you are studying cells or circuits, pupils still need to be able to use analogies, and if they can't yet, that is your chance to get out the analogy cards and move the learning on.

It is sometimes a case of being persistent. If you feel that you have tried everything and still are not being used successfully in particular lessons, it is appropriate to suggest to your manager that you may be of more use elsewhere. But it is more likely that once the teachers realise you have a lot to contribute, they will be keen to include you in their lessons.

Once you feel confident enough to work with a small group of pupils, it is worth discussing with the teacher that you are happy to take larger groups; many teachers may assume that you would be uncomfortable with this. As you become confident at working with larger groups, you can experiment with different pupil groups in different situations. For example, you could take charge of most of the class as they carry out an activity while the class teacher works intensively with a smaller group of pupils who are making slower progress. Where occasionally splitting the class like this has become an established way of working between pupils, teachers and teaching assistants, it can be extremely effective.

Knowing that the teaching assistant is confident enough to take a group of pupils through an activity can also be useful where the activity requires different groups to be working with quite a different focus, or where particular individuals work better apart from each other. It increases flexibility within the classroom and makes for more successful learning.

Taking it further for your department

If you have a teacher you are working with very successfully you could ask the Head of Department for a slot in a departmental meeting to 'share good practice'. Choose the resource you think is most effective at moving on learners in your classes and share it with the department. When you are sharing good practice, there is a tried and tested way to do it that makes an impact. Keep it brief; don't take longer than eight or ten minutes. Although you will have used the resource in a particular context or topic, emphasise the skills and the transferability of the strategy.

State the problem you identified – give an example – share your solution – give an evaluation.

Use these stages to present your work to the department.

■ First, describe the common problem or issue you identified for a pupil or a group of pupils. For example, 'I noticed that a group of pupils in 11G were really struggling with their write-up'.

■ Second, describe the problem, giving an example with a pupil name if possible. For example, 'When I spoke to Paul, Rosie and Tim in Mrs. Finnis's class, it turned out they didn't really understand the vocabulary of the mark guidance – when it mentioned reliability, they didn't know what that was'.

■ Third, describe your solution and then show how it is used. For example, 'This cube has a coursework key word and a series of questions on each side. It can be used to start a conversation with the pupils about what the words mean and whether they have used them correctly in their write up. I've used it to circulate around the whole class and make sure they are on track while Mrs. Finnis has been working with a small group that needed extra support.'

■ Lastly, pass round the resource and describe the responses from the pupils. If possible, give a specific example of a pupil and the response. You could tell the department the difference the resource had made to the pupil's marks for the evaluation section.

Teachers are very busy people, but they know a good thing when they see it!

I predict teachers will be enthusiastic for a resource when you present it in this way. Make sure you have a few electronic or hard copies at the ready because teachers will want to take them away and use them soon. This solution-focused approach will start to build your reputation as an effective practitioner with great ideas. Nothing is more effective than a solution-focused approach in building respect among staff and pupils.

Taking it further for your school

Once the science department has a teaching assistant that is attached to the department, and the other departments see how powerful such a model can be, other departments will tend to request the same thing. This can be an amazing opportunity to raise the profile of the science department within the school and spread the good practice that you and the science department have begun.

Don't be afraid to talk about what you do. Team up with your Head of Department or a teacher with whom you work well and put together a presentation to deliver at a school Leadership Team meeting, or even a Governors meeting. Some examples of the sort of thing that can be effective are included on the CD provided with this book. You can personalise them for your department and particular way of working. Make sure you are clear about the things that need to be in place for the teaching assistant to transform the learning in science classrooms. If the SENCO had a flexible approach, and this enabled a more creative way of working, then acknowledge it. The Leadership Team may not be aware of the blockers to good practice that have been overcome in the science department but that still exist elsewhere in the school.

Taking it even further...

It may be appropriate to take your show on the road; to share good practice with other local schools, or to visit schools where teaching assistant support works well and you'd like to glean some more ideas to support your own work. Another possibility that would raise the profile of teaching assistants and support the development of good practice may be to form a teaching assistant network in your area. The internet, of course, is an extremely powerful tool in this respect and a forum or emailing group can be established with relative ease.

Becoming a Higher Level Teaching Assistant in England (HLTA)

This is becoming an increasingly popular route for teaching assistants in England who wish to expand further their role and profile within the school, increase the amount of responsibility they have and develop their classroom practice. Your Local Authority will have received funding to train a number of a science HLTAs; if this is a route you would like to pursue, get in touch with them. Other teaching assistants may decide to opt for classroom teaching, whether in a primary or secondary setting, or may go into adult education, either as a learner or as a tutor.

There is general information on becoming an HLTA on the Training and Development for Schools website:
http://www.tda.gov.uk/support/hlta.aspx

And specific information about becoming a science HLTA here:
http://www.tda.gov.uk/support/hlta/maths_science_hlta.aspx

A pilot study carried out in 2005–2006 showed the positive impact of HLTAs on pupils, relationships between teachers and the HLTA, and reducing teacher workload (TDA, 2007). Within Cornwall Local Authority I have been involved with the training for HLTAs. The HLTAs that I have worked with have been very positive about their role. They opted for HLTA training because they felt it gave them the opportunity to enhance their status within the department and to improve their specialist subject knowledge. Almost all the HLTAs I have spoken to commented that the training had really improved their confidence in the classroom, and given a much clearer understanding of progression.

Some HLTAs commented that more guidance should be given to schools and classroom teachers about how HLTAs can be used to support learning – many would like to have more responsibility. A model of working that seems to work extremely well is to have an HLTA leading a team of teaching assistants. The HLTA has a good understanding of the issues facing the teaching assistants, but also has a more strategic view of the departmental needs and how these can best be met by the team.

Summary of chapter 5

There are a number of ways to spread effective practice through a department and school.

Some staff will be 'enthusiasts' and will work closely with you. Use their enthusiasm and insight do develop an effective way of working together.

- Use staff meetings as an opportunity to share the good practice that you are developing with other members of the department.

- For maximum impact when sharing good practice, use the model 'State the problem – give an example – share a solution – give an evaluation' to illustrate the way you are working with learners.

- As your confidence builds, volunteer to share your good practice more widely: to other departments in the school and to other schools.

Becoming a Higher Level Teaching Assistant (HLTA)

- Teaching assistants who would like a higher profile in the department or school, or who would like more responsibility and the chance of higher pay may choose to train to become a HLTA.

- Funding is available from Local Authorities for teaching assistants in science to train as HLTAs.

- HLTAs report that they have much more confidence in the classroom as a result of HLTA training, and in many cases this led to increased enjoyment and job satisfaction.

The last big idea

'Education is the most powerful weapon which you can use to change the world.'
Nelson Mandela

Whatever you decide to do with your career, remember that you do make a difference.

With your experience, with your ideas and with your enthusiasm, and armed with the strategies from this book, you will move learning on for the young people with whom you work.

You make a difference to their education, and you make a difference to their chances in life.

Enjoy it – and from the young people who you support in the classroom – thank you.

Jo Foster

Bibliography

Blatchford, P., Martin, C., Moriarty, V., Bassett, P., Goldstein, H. (2002) *Pupil: adult ratio differences and educational progress over Reception and Key Stage 1*, London: DfES

Blatchford, P., Russell, A., Bassett, P., Brown, P. and Martin, C. (2004) *The role and effects of teaching assistants in English primary schools (years 4–6)*, London: DfES

Cajkler, W., Tennant, G., Tiknaz, Y., Sage, R., Tucker, S. and Taylor, C. (2007) A systematic literature review on how training and professional development activities impact on teaching assistants' classroom practice (1988–2006), *Research Evidence in Education Library*, London: EPPI-Centre, Social Science Research Unit, Institute of Education, University of London

Gerber, S., Finn, J., Achilles, C. and Boyd-Zaharias, J. (2001) Teacher aides and students' academic achievement, *Educational Evaluation and Policy Analysis*, **23**, 2

Giangreco, M.F., Edelman, S., Luiselli, T.E., and MacFarland, S.Z. (1997) Helping or hovering? Effects of instructional assistant proximity on students with disabilities. *Exceptional Children*, **64** (1), 7–18

Hawkins, P. (1999) *The Art of Building Windmills: Career Tactics for the 21st Century*, New edition, Graduate into Employment Unit

Howes, A., Farrell, P., Kaplan, I. and Moss, S. (2003) The impact of paid adult support on the participation and learning of pupils in mainstream schools, *Research Evidence in Education Library*, London: EPPI-Centre, Social Science Research Unit, Institute of Education, University of London

Nind, M., Simmons, K., Sheehy, K. and Rix, J. (2004) *Inclusive Education: Learners and Learning Contexts*, UK: Routledge

Smith, P., Whitby, K. and Sharp, C. (2004) *The Employment and Deployment of Teaching Assistants*, (LGA Research report 5/04) Slough: NFER

Training and Development Agency (2007) Higher Level Teaching Assistant: *Secondary Mathematics and Science, Pilot research summary and programme update*

Tennant, G. (2001) The rhetoric and reality of learning support in the classroom: towards a synthesis, *Support for Learning*, **16**, 4, 184–8

Wilson, R., Sharp, C., Shuayb, M., Kendall, L., Wade, P. and Easton, C. (2007) *Research into the deployment and impact of support staff who have achieved HLTA status. Final Report*, Slough: NFER

Index

Teaching Assistants' Box of Tricks CD with e-resources

The documents on this CD enable you to select any of the e-resource pages in the printed book for reproduction for use in your classroom. Download the files to your computer desktop and use them as copymasters or for display on an interactive whiteboard. You can use the pdf documents as copymasters. The PowerPoint documents allow you to download the resources and edit the text on the page to suit your pupils.

Contents list for documents on CD